Negotiating
in Asia

Content of this book is based on four decades of work experience negotiating in Asian countries. Although every precaution has been taken to provide accurate information herein, the author and publisher assume no responsibility for any errors or omissions. No liability is assumed for damages that may result from the use of information contained within. Likewise web links in this book were live at the time of publishing but may become inactive or change over time.

Books may be purchased in quantity by contacting the publisher at info@writewaypublishingcompany.com.

Printed in the United States of America

First Edition
ISBN 978-1-946425-21-8

Library of Congress Control Number: 2018955088

Front cover concept by Robert Charles Azar
Cover Design by CSinclaire Write-Design
Book Design by CSinclaire Write-Design

Cover art ©: www.123rf.com/profile_lehui'>lehui/123RFstockphoto</a>

What Readers Are Saying...

"A thorough East Asian hand, Robert Azar has worthy counsel for newcomers and those experienced in negotiations with firms and others in that part of the world.... Basic to a successful deal is knowledge of how those across the table customarily think and operate, notably when it is different from how we do."

John Sylvester II
Former Deputy Director of the Office of Research and Analysis on East Asia
U.S. Department of State

"The economies of Asia and the United States are increasingly intertwined. Unique challenges faced by US executives in Asia are actually opportunities for educated and informed businesspeople. Robert's timely discussion of cross-border negotiations—from his very practical viewpoint—is just such an educational tool, transforming unfamiliar situations into golden opportunities."

David S. Robinson, Esq.
Honorary General Consul of Japan in Raleigh, North Carolina, 2015-present

"Robert Azar draws on nearly forty years of experience to write a book for anyone planning to engage in business negotiations with a business headquartered in Asia. With an emphasis on the most critical dynamics of international negotiation, Azar describes the cultural values common to Japan, Korea, and China as well as the differences among the three (and they are significant).

"Smartly, Azar also emphasizes the importance of thoughtful planning in advance of a negotiation session, the context of a negotiation that could make an American negotiator vulnerable in a negotiation, and above all the importance of using a "facilitator interpreter" for the negotiation.

"Regardless of the depth and breadth of experience a novice or seasoned executive might possess, the insights and advice that Azar provides in this book will be immensely helpful as he/she prepares for the exciting opportunity to partner with a business in Asia."

Scott Buechler, Ph.D.
Former Associate Dean
The Martha and Spencer Love School of Business
Elon University
Emeritus Associate Professor of Business Communications

"Robert Azar has produced an invaluable compendium for anyone interested in understanding the complex process of negotiating across cultures, in this instance the multi-faceted Asian culture.... Mr. Azar's outstanding volume contains a plethora of essential, insightful, critical and highly useful information that, once assimilated, can help us perform more effectively in this increasingly important global domain."

Thomas J. White
Director, Economic Development Partnership, North Carolina State University
Former President & CEO, Durham, North Carolina Chamber of Commerce

"The practice of negotiation varies from nation to nation. This is especially true regarding what the other country's negotiators are thinking and seek to achieve. This book does an outstanding job of enabling Americans and Asians to more fully understand each other's approach and the built-in but unspoken business aims and cultural expectations. As a Japanese executive who negotiates with American companies and in other countries, this book helps me as a reference and guide."

Kyoichi Okamoto
President & CEO, Morinaga America Foods, Inc.

"This book provides essential information for successfully negotiating in Asia. As a former student of Prof. Azar, I have benefited tremendously from his deep insights into Asian business, especially regarding strategies for success in differing business cultures. This book conveys this valuable and practical information with great readability."

Jack Dudek, student
Martha & Spencer Love School of Business
Elon University

Negotiating in Asia

A Practical Guide to Succeeding in International Negotiations

Robert Charles Azar

Write Way Publishing Company

Other Books by the Author

Navigating Japan's Business Culture:
A Practical Guide to Succeeding in the Japanese Market

Insightful Thoughts for the Journey Through Life
Original messages of insight and inspiration
combining Eastern wisdoms and Western philosophy

CONTENTS

Chapter 3
NEGOTIATION PROTOCOLS

PART TWO: CRITICAL ROLE OF COMMUNICATION

Chapter 4
COMMUNICATION DYNAMICS:
The Stealth Determinant

Chapter 5

CRITICAL ROLE OF THE FACILITATOR INTERPRETER:

Interpreting Beyond Language and Beyond Language Interpreting

PART THREE: ADDITIONAL STRATEGIES FOR SUCCESS

Chapter 6

FURTHER NEGOTIATING CONSIDERATIONS

LIST OF FIGURES AND TABLES

FIGURES

TABLE

INTRODUCTION

When clients would inquire in the early stages of my career about what is dissimilar when it comes to negotiating in Asia, I would reply by mentioning one or two major differences. Over time, as the length of my career working firsthand in Asian markets changed from being counted in years to being measured in decades, my reply included an ever-increasing number of factors. After nearly four decades of negotiating business deals in Asia for American and European clients, the number of differences has become a substantial list. Here are twenty-five aspects of negotiating that differ in Asia from common Western practices. Each is a major, representative difference with the diversity in the list indicating how fundamental and far reaching these dissimilarities are.

1. *Views* of negotiating
2. *Purpose* of negotiating
3. *Approach* to negotiating
4. *Goals* in negotiating
5. *Priorities* in negotiating
6. *Dynamics* governing negotiations

7. Degree of importance given to the *other party's interests*
8. *Timing* for presenting negotiation objectives
9. *How* negotiating objectives are presented
10. *Protocols* informing negotiations
11. Dealing with *differences* in bargaining positions
12. *Depth of information* disclosed in negotiations
13. Degree of *compromise* necessary in negotiations
14. *Decision-making* in negotiations
15. Use of *third parties*
16. *Length* of negotiations
17. *Pace* of negotiations
18. *Frequency* of negotiation meetings
19. *Communication dynamics* informing negotiations
20. *Conflict* resolution processes
21. *Time horizons utilized* in negotiations
22. *Geographic location* of negotiation meetings
23. Appropriate *venue* for negotiation dialogue
24. *Participants* selected to attend negotiating meetings
25. *Seating arrangement significance* during negotiations

Each and every one of these differences presents a potent and ever-present challenge to American companies engaging in negotiating in Asia. Like the portion of the proverbial iceberg beneath the surface, these challenges generally lurk unseen and unrecognized by Western executives. However, make no mistake about it—they are there. Their impact ranges from minor to major, nuanced to causal. Accordingly, when not sufficiently understood and prepared for, Western companies shortchange their negotiating efforts; they enter the negotiating room at not only a strategic disadvantage but a tactical one as well.

These negotiating differences impact foreign businesses in

Asian markets in a profound manner. In a best-case scenario, the level of success American firms attain in negotiating is curtailed. In a worse-case scenario, their negotiations or their post-negotiation business outright fails.

One only needs to look at what the word "negotiating" actually means in various countries to quickly see how the practice of negotiating is viewed, approached, and engaged in differently around the world.

For example, in English the Latin root of negotiating is *negotiatus,* which means *"to carry on business."* As Americans, we tend to view negotiating as transactional and a means to an end— an activity to advance one's business interests that will allow us to *carry on our business* with other companies. Accordingly, we engage in negotiating in a direct, deliberate, and straightforward manner.

In contrast, negotiating in Japan, for instance, is anything but transactional or a simple means to an end. Nor is it just an activity solely to carry on one's business. Rather the central goal of negotiation in Japan is comprised of dual facets:

- *To associate with* and get to know the other party to see if a trust relationship can be built between the parties

- To see if it is possible for both parties to *be involved* in working together to enhance their mutual interests for the long term through cooperating on the business project under consideration

The word for negotiating in the Japanese language clearly expresses this different meaning of negotiating. The word *kou-shou* (交渉) means *"to associate with, to go across, to involve."* Accordingly, negotiating is different parties associating with, going across to the other party's side to get to know their business interests and needs and thereby identifying mutual interests. It is committing to be involved in securing those mutual interests over the long term through a trust relationship. Once this is understood, it should come as no surprise that the role of relationship in negotiating is as central as it is in Japan and throughout most of Asia.

In China, the word for negotiating is *tán pàn* (谈判). The first character means *"to discuss"* and the second one *"to judge."* Accordingly, negotiating is seen as the means *to discuss a matter to enable a judgment* as to whether or not one can engage in business with the other party. In this way, negotiating in China is utilitarian, a means to a specific end similar to negotiating in the U.S.

In the Korean language, the word for negotiating is *hyeob-sang hada* (협상하다) and means *"to decide, settle, and fix."* Consequently, a negotiation is expected to have a definitive outcome that *decides a matter, settles the situation, and fixes specific terms.* As you might expect from this meaning, final decisions are often made on the spot during initial negotiating meetings, and negotiations in Korea proceed much faster than in other Asian markets.

In Thailand, the word for negotiating is *"dtòr rong."* *"Dtor"* means *"to bargain"* or *"to haggle,"* while *"rong"* means *"to carry, bear, or support."* Negotiating is approached as *the haggling activity one bears in order to bargain* for a desired result.

The Indonesian term for negotiating is *"perundingan,"* which is *a palaver or long parley.* As negotiations are an *opportunity to consult and discuss at length*, they are expected to be long with no expectation of agreement being reached right away.

The Malaysian word for negotiaton is *"rundingan"* and means *"talks."* It is the *opportunity to converse and exchange information.* There is no rush to make a decision or finalize a deal.

In contrast to conversing and exchanging information, in Vietnam the word for negotiate, *"dam-phan,"* means *to trade or deal*—clearly more transaction-oriented with an expectation for quicker conclusion and definitive outcome.

This pattern of the word "negotiating" carrying different meanings, goals, approaches, and nuances from country to country goes beyond America and Asia.

In Germany, the word for negotiating is *"verhandlung"* and means *"to discuss or debate."* As you would anticipate, logical reasoning, facts, and figures weigh heavily rather than relationship considerations when negotiating there.

The Italian word for negotiating, *"trattativa,"* means *"to talk and deal."* Accordingly, negotiations in that country are very roundabout with considerable talking, schmoozing, and dealing making.

In Spain, the term for negotiating is *"negociacion"* and means *"to bargain and transact."* As a result, negotiating there tends to be more straightforward and transaction oriented.

In Brazil, *"negociacao"* means *"to deal, settle, or enroll."* Thus, negotiating entails lots of discussion and persuasion *to enroll the other party and settle upon a deal.*

As we have seen, what it means to negotiate varies significantly country to country—anywhere from simply talking to exchanging information to persuading, haggling, bargaining, or making a deal to moving one's own business agenda forward to establishing a trust relationship and committing to both parties' mutual interests for the long term.

As the very *meaning and purpose* of negotiation varies so widely around the world, it is only natural that the *practice* of negotiating likewise differs country to country.

What are the specifics that create these different practices of negotiating around the globe? Negotiations are impacted by numerous environments that influence business in each country. The following eight are some of these major environments:

- A nation's political system

- The legal and regulatory requirements of a country

- The country's level of economic development

- The level of development of the industries of the negotiating parties

- The size and competitive standing of each company in its industry

- The degree of wealth of the people of a nation

- The historical experience of countries

- The cultural norms and societal expectations of a market

The first seven of these environments are generally well-known, and there are numerous sources of information on them. Consequently, rather than addressing these topics and repeating already known facts, this book focuses on the role that culture-based differences in business practices play in international negotiating and presents new understanding regarding them. Culture is a factor that remains all too often overlooked both in global negotiating and in business in general.

Ever-quicker advances in recent technologies have resulted in the world seemingly becoming a smaller place. The emergence of the "global village" has made it possible for people, companies, and countries to become much closer, more easily communicated with, and accessed with an ease never experienced before in human history. We have even seen the emergence of a "global consumer culture"—world famous brands, products, and concepts such as Starbucks, anime, Apple, feng shui, Coach, and sushi—that seemingly transcends national cultures. As a result, many assert that the importance of cultural differences in global business is steadily diminishing. However, speaking from first-hand experience, the reality is quite the opposite.

The importance of culture-based differences in business practices has only become more significant in recent times. The closer proximity and immediate response time that technology has afforded brings those differences even closer to home. They have become issues that workers now deal with on a daily basis in ever more multi-cultural work teams as well as with conference calls, emails, international Skype meetings, and other communications between company affiliates and business partners around the world.

Likewise, here at home in America, we see the daily challenges of cultural differences within companies as they struggle to create an effective, in-house "corporate culture" that seeks to deal with the challenges of culture-based differences in business practices *right here in their own domestic locations* in America. Whereas previously, culture-based differences in business practices only influenced a firm's international business operations on the other side of oceans, now they impact operations at home as well other locations in this interconnected age of the global village.

Furthermore, whereas previously greater amounts of time and distance helped to buffer and thereby mitigate cultural differences, technological advances have brought culture-based differences in business practices to the foreground of business interactions. They are a more direct and immediate factor in business than ever before. An integral part of business today, companies can no longer afford to ignore culture-based differences in business practices. Yet they remain one of the most overlooked and underappreciated aspects of business. This book provides new insights into how companies can attain greater success in negotiating and running their businesses in today's hyperconnected, global environment.

The primary goal of this book is to elucidate the differences in the art and practice of negotiating both internationally and interculturally. This book provides proven insights and strategies, honed over nearly four decades of firsthand experience in the trenches of international business, that will enable the reader to more effectively negotiate across national boundaries and cultural barriers. While its primary focus is Asia, the reader will benefit from its information, perspectives, and lessons when negotiating in other geographic areas as well, as he/she will have learned what negotiating factors are generally different, examples of how they are dissimilar, and how one might successfully navigate them.

The book initially provides a two-point comparison contrasting how negotiating is engaged in differently in America and Asia. Going beyond that common two-dimensional contrast, this book then provides a third dimension of comparison by showing how the practice of negotiating varies among the three largest economies in Asia—China, Japan, and South Korea. This book is unique for demonstrating not only how negotiating is practiced so differently between America and Asia but also how negotiating is practiced differently among Asian nations themselves in both nuance and substance. Additionally, going beyond simply presenting *descriptions* of those important differences, the book provides *proven strategies and tactics* for successfully dealing with those differences.

Unless otherwise noted, the information and insights contained in this book are factual and based on firsthand experience. The negotiating practices described in each country are what is mainstream. It is acknowledged that not every company or individual swims in the mainstream. In addition, regional as well as generational differences in each country may also result in variations to what is mainstream. Accordingly, this book serves as a baseline from which variations in negotiating within each country profiled can be further delineated.

The names of companies, employees, and products of American and Asian companies that I have worked with have been changed out of respect for their privacy. The names of historical companies, individuals, and products, however, have not been altered. The names of Asian individuals are written family name first, followed by their first name in accord with Asian tradition.

This book will be of interest to and benefit three groups of readers. In the first group are individuals with professional interests in Asia, such as those in business and government. The second is comprised of those with an academic interest in both Asia and negotiating in general, such as teachers and students of both Asian business and Asian culture. The third group constitutes the culturally curious and globally minded who are interested in the many diverse cultures that enrich our world as well as those seeking greater cross-cultural competence. It is my hope that this book will foster greater global prosperity, understanding, and peace by enabling individuals, companies, and countries to better understand each other and more effectively negotiate across national boundaries and cultural barriers.

Robert Charles Azar
Cary, North Carolina
U.S.A.
October 2018

PART ONE

APPROACHES, DYNAMICS, AND PROTOCOLS

CHAPTER 1

CONTENDING APPROACHES TO NEGOTIATING:

East vs. West

Negotiating, as well as business in general, is viewed, approached, and engaged in with styles, goals, protocols, and dynamics in America that differ in both nuance and substance from the rest of the world. Let's look at some of the major differences in the practice of negotiating between the U.S. and Asia.

I. NEGOTIATING U.S. STYLE

Historically, the traditional American approach to negotiating is known as *positional bargaining*. In this style of negotiating, each party advocates for its position on each item being negotiated.

The goal of negotiating is to win agreement from the other side to as many of the terms that your firm desires as you can while ceding as few as possible. In the U.S. approach to negotiating, it is acceptable that one party's gain in the negotiation is the other party's loss. Consequently, it is often characterized as being a *zero-sum game*. Here are six major traits of American positional style negotiating.

First, the focus of positional negotiating is on the interests of one's own company. This style of negotiating does not give priority to the interests of the other party. Because of this, it can be said that the focus of American negotiating is singular—gaining your company's objectives.

This negotiating method does not give priority to enabling the other party to obtain what they are aiming for through the negotiation. In short, Company A is not much concerned with the impact on Company B as Company A works to secure agreement on its own negotiation objectives. The reverse is also true. Company B does not consider the implications on Company A when Company B is working to secure its own negotiating positions. Instead, in positional bargaining, each party focuses on its own needs and objectives—its own positions—without much regard for the impact on the other party.

Second, not only is positional bargaining unconcerned with the needs of the other party, it also results in companies achieving their corporate interests at the expense of the other party. It is based on a "we" versus "them" premise, approach, and dynamic—my win is your loss. Or, as it is often expressed by negotiators, "what is mine is mine, and what is yours is mine."

Third, relationship does not have a prominent role in positional negotiating. In fact, relationship plays little, if any, role in this negotiating style. As will be discussed in detail in chapter two, focusing on relationship is often seen as detrimental to achieving optimal success in negotiations as well as to the negotiators themselves.

U.S. companies without a prior relationship and therefore who are unknown to each other commonly engage in negotiations and, if successful, commence business together with relationship having no part in the process. As a result, how negotiations commence or are conducted will not be impacted by matters related to relationship. Consequently, positional negotiating is not influenced by concerns about or efforts in the area of relationship building. This is quite different in Asian negotiating where relationship plays a central role in how negotiations are initiated, conducted, and culminated. Chapter two explores this dynamic and critically important difference.

Fourth, in positional bargaining, negotiations start with a fixed list of topics to be covered. That is, the items to be included in the negotiation are determined before the beginning of the negotiation. This is typically done in advance before the parties meet to negotiate. These topics become the fixed agenda for the negotiations. The items included in the fixed agenda represent the total universe of topics that the parties will negotiate, often referred to as the "value pie." The goal of each party is to divide up that fixed value pie so as to gain as much of it as possible for themselves.

Since the aim of the negotiation is to divide up or distribute the value pie between the participating parties, positional negotiating is also known as *distributive negotiating*.

Fifth, in positional negotiating, a company avoids divulging up front their bottom line position for each topic of the negotiation. The company's target goals are often padded to allow for bargaining. As a result, it is expected that the padded number will be negotiated and come close to the company's bottom line position. Accordingly, bargaining and even haggling are dynamics that are included in positional negotiating.

For instance, you are negotiating with a company whose product you wish to buy. Their usual transfer price is $100 per unit. However, your desired purchase price for their product is $95 per unit. In positional bargaining, you would start the discussion of that item by proposing a price of $90, allowing for the other party to counter with a price slightly lower than their original one. You bargain back and forth until reaching a price acceptable for both parties as near to your desired $95 price as possible.

The guideline commonly used to describe this approach is "holding your cards close to the vest." In fact, so well established is this notion in American negotiating that one of the well-known principles of positional bargaining is that "the party that speaks first loses," since it is understood that once a position is clearly stated, it will be countered with a weaker one by the other party as a matter of course.

Sixth, since one party's gain is the other's loss, positional bargaining is a "winner takes all" style for negotiating each item of the negotiation. This approach has a profound effect on American style negotiating, including in the following six fundamental areas:

- The *goal* of negotiating

- The manner in which each party to the negotiation *views and relates to the other*

- Each company's *approach* to negotiating

- The *methods* used by each party

- The *dynamics* that govern negotiating

- The role and importance of *relationship* in negotiating

These differences and how they impact the practice of negotiation in America and Asia are examined throughout this book.

Positional or distributive bargaining has long been the primary form of negotiating in the United States and still is prevalent. However, in 1981 Robert Fisher, William Ury, and Bruce Patton published *Getting to YES: Negotiating Agreement Without Giving In*. This book had a significant impact on American negotiating by introducing a novel approach and offering an alternative driving dynamic of negotiating.

Getting to YES: Negotiating Agreement Without Giving In advocates that, rather than positional or distributive bargaining, negotiators should utilize *integrative negotiating*. In contrast to positional bargaining's focus on dividing up the fixed value pie, integrative negotiating involves adding or integrating new items of interest or value to the negotiations as they may arise during the course of the negotiations. By so doing, negotiators can, instead of pushing for their own positions in a winner-take-all manner, seek to win the agreement of the other party on some items by allowing the other party to win some of the new areas of interest or value that are added. Conversely, in exchange for the points of interest your firm ceded to the other party, your company can win agreement for some of the newly added value items.

> The dynamic of negotiating is modified from being strictly win-lose.

In short, by adding new areas of value or interest that are identified during the course of the negotiation and dividing them up, integrative negotiating allows both parties to more easily accept tradeoffs and make concessions. As a result, the dynamic of negotiating is modified from being strictly win-lose or *zero-sum game* to allowing for some degree of mutual winning in the negotiation.

The shift from positional to integrative negotiating changed the U.S. approach from dividing the prefixed value pie to enlarging it by adding new items of value and then dividing it. The Harvard University Law School's Program on Negotiating, widely considered to be one of America's leaders in negotiation training, likewise advocates this approach to negotiating. They refer to it as *principled negotiation* or *negotiation on the merits*.*

II. ASIAN APPROACH TO NEGOTIATING

Negotiating is engaged in with a very different premise and approach in Asia.

* For further reading: Harvard Business Essentials. *Negotiating*. Cambridge, MA: Harvard Business Review Press, 2003.

First, unlike positional negotiating where a company's sole focus is on their own corporate interest, the interests of both parties are acknowledged, openly discussed, and pursued in Asian negotiations.

> The interests of both parties are acknowledged, openly discussed, and pursued in Asian negotiations

Second, avoiding the achiev-ing of one's own interests at the expense of other party—the "we versus them" dynamic common in the States—Asian negotiating instead operates with the goal of arriving at decisions that are win-win for both parties. This is in stark contrast to the *zero-sum game* nature of positional negotiating or integrative negotiation's ceding new items of value to the other party if they can be identified during the course of the negotiation. In Asia, negotiating and business are viewed as a process of give and take in which both companies recognize and try to accommodate each other's business interests while endeavoring to secure the long-term success of the joint business project.

Third, negotiating and business are seen as being based on the relationship that the parties either have before negotiations com-mence or build during the negotiation process. Relationship is both the foundation upon which negotiating and business are conducted and the framework within which negotiating and business are con-ducted. Whereas relationship has little role in U.S. negotiating, it is paramount in Asia. This theme is examined throughout this book.

Fourth, rather than seeking to distribute the fixed items of value set out at the beginning of the negotiation, Asian nego-tiators see all topics and interests as being organically interrelated. As agreement is made on topics, it is believed that subsequent items will be affected and, therefore, changed. It is not possible to "fix" the entire list of topics or value items. Instead, they remain open to deal with them as they may evolve throughout the course of the negotiation.

Fifth, given the approach of openly taking into consideration each other's interests, Asian negotiators are more apt to let their true business interests and bottom line positions be known to the other party earlier rather than later in the negotiating process. It would not be possible to discuss each party's interests without doing so. This is quite different from the positional bargaining tactic to avoid divulging one's bottom line positions up front and "keeping your cards close to your vest."

Sixth, as negotiations and business are based on relationships and promoting mutual interests, the "winner takes all" approach of U.S. style negotiating is not desirable in much of Asia. Negotiating that gives priority to relationship is seen as the best way for each side to achieve the greatest number of their respective business interests not only in negotiating the business project at hand but also for their broader corporate interests over the long term.

What accounts for these numerous, fundamental, and far-reaching differences in negotiating in Asia?

What accounts for these numerous, fundamental, and far-reaching differences in negotiating in Asia? What is the cause of this radically different approach to negotiating and business? The cause is that what drives business in America and Asia is fundamentally different. Let's get specific.

In America, business is *trans-action or purpose driven*. That is, two or more companies agree to collaborate to achieve the specific business objectives of a clearly specified project or transaction. Those goals are carefully and comprehensively delineated in the business agreement the com-

> What drives business in America and Asia is fundamentally different.

panies sign in order to start a project. These agreements spell out the specific roles and responsibilities of each party in great detail, and by signing the agreement, the companies commit themselves to performing those specified tasks. They are not responsible for or obligated to provide any work or services beyond what the agreement specifically calls on them to do. Nor is it expected that they will work together beyond the scope and time of the project specified in the agreement.

In the same way, positional and integrative negotiations also are transaction or purpose driven. Accordingly, they focus narrowly on the specific business objectives and topics of the value pie as it may or may not change over the course of the negotiation.

In contrast, business in Asia is *relationship driven*. Business is engaged in based on the foundation of the relationship between the companies involved. While it is possible in America for companies previously unknown to each other to start conducting business together by simply putting in place a clearly defined business agreement, that is uncommon in Asia. There companies generally do not work together without a relationship because mutual collaboration promotes both the mutual business interests of each company and their shared relationship. While American business is purpose driven and, by extension, so is our negotiating focus, Asian business is relationship driven and, by the same token, so is their approach to negotiating. In this way, while purpose takes precedence over relationship in U.S. negotiating and business, relationship takes precedence in Asia.

As a consequence of this preference, negotiating in Asia takes place in these three distinct areas:

- Learning about and confirming the parameters of the joint business project

- Coming to agreement on the specifics of the joint business venture

- Creating a sense of partnership and mutual benefit between the two firms by building a cooperative relationship

American executives are well acquainted with the first two of these areas of negotiating—learning about and confirming the parameters of the project and coming to agreement on the specifics of the joint business venture. However, the third aspect of relationship building is not given much importance in American business culture. As relationship commands central importance in business in Asia, it is imperative that American executives prepare themselves to engage in effective relationship building and long-term relationship maintenance.

It is important to note that Asian companies pursue these three areas of negotiating simultaneously and in parallel. This is the reason so much relationship building activity occurs during the course of the negotiations and one of the reasons that negotiations proceed more slowly and take longer in Asia than in the West.

In Asia, relationship not only plays a crucial role in negotiations and business but also has far greater longevity than in the U.S. In the States, once the purpose of the mutual transaction is completed, the parties wish each other well and go their separate ways. In other words, business is generally *short term* in nature and so is any relationship that may have developed between the companies. By contrast, it is not unusual for the mutual relationship to outlast individual business projects in Asian markets; in short, the mutual business relationship often survives the mutual business project.

> In Asian markets, the mutual business relationship often survives the mutual business project.

This is especially true in Japan where both companies commit to work together to enhance their mutual interests and well-being *long term*—through the initial business project as well as subsequent ones over time that are not contemplated at the initial negotiation.

In this way, establishing and maintaining a favorable mutual relationship is a deliberate best business practice that plants seeds for future business opportunities with trusted partners and, consequently, pays a long-term return on investment. That is why the practice of investing significant time, effort, and resources in business relationships is valued as highly as it is in Asian nations.

Given the centrality of relationship in business, Asian cultures have long placed great importance and priority on them. Relationships are highly valued and taken very seriously. This is why Asians are quite formal and polite in relating to others. In addition, the degree of formality and politeness does not diminish with the passage of time; instead it is observed by all parties concerned out of respect for the individuals in the other companies as well as respect for the mutual relationship between those individuals and their companies.

In America, by contrast, we tend to take relationships much more lightly and relate to each other informally. So commonplace is this that we are comfortable with being casual even with those we meet for the very first time. For example, we are quick to call each other by first name. We commonly use humor to foster a more relaxed, informal, and friendly atmosphere in meetings. We are quick to invite everyone in the room to get comfortable and take off their suit jackets. This is not the case in Asia, where one is expected to remain formal and respectful in relationships, both in negotiating and in business.

Contrary to American tendencies, first names are rarely used in business in Asia; first names are used only with family members and close social friends. Even when employees have worked together for decades, they still call each other by family name, not by their given name. To convey this preference for formality even more accurately, individuals in leadership roles or positions of authority are often called by their title, not even their name. For example, the president of a company will be addressed as "President" (*sha-cho* 社長 in Japanese). A manager will be addressed as "Manager" (*bu-cho* 部長). This is done out of respect not only for (1) the individual person but also for

(2) their position and (3) the relationship an employee has with each superior. Respect is thus shown on all three levels and done so simultaneously—rather novel from an American perspective. This is another indication of how highly valued, respected, and important relationships are in Asian business cultures.

It is imperative that American executives realize just how important relationship is in Asia. American companies will achieve greater success in negotiating when they give relationships the attention they require. The failure to do so negatively impacts negotiations from simply slowing them down to outright causing them to fail. I have witnessed numerous occasions where American and European companies' negotiations were dragged out or irreparably damaged due to their inability or failure to successfully navigate relationship dynamics with potential Asian partners.

> It is imperative that American executives realize just how important relationship is in Asia.

I have long advised clients to think of these two parts of negotiating—relationship building and clarifying and agreeing upon the specifics of the project—as the two tracks of a railroad. A train can only move forward if both tracks are laid at the same time. In addition, both tracks must be put in place parallel. Likewise, negotiations with Asian companies will only move forward when progress in both project discussion and relationship building occur in tandem. Specifically, Asian companies must reach a comfort level with both the specifics of the proposed business venture as well as the development of the relationship simultaneously. As a general rule, Asian businesses are hesitant to embark on a business venture with a new partner without a sufficient comfort level in both areas.

As we have seen, the Asian approach to negotiation incorporates four distinct features:

- Identifying and working in good faith toward the mutual interests of the parties involved in the immediate project under discussion from the outset of the negotiation and continuously throughout

- Continuously factoring into the negotiation the broader corporate interests of the parties

- Respecting, valuing, and continuously promoting throughout the entire negotiation the mutual relationship between the parties

- Possessing and demonstrating a long-term commitment to the above three

While present in varying degrees throughout Asian markets, they are factors that are unique to negotiation in Asia and not present in American negotiating. They indicate the wider scope of Asian negotiating and the broader purview within which Asian executives negotiate.

In Asian markets, this four-fold approach to negotiating and business is significantly more inclusive, mutual-benefit oriented, and broader-based in focus than the positional or integrative bargaining of the U.S. It is, therefore, not unusual for the goals and needs of the mutual business project and the negotiating parties to be discussed at great length throughout the course of the negotiations. In fact, the broader goals and needs of the mutual business project and the negotiating parties are sometimes given even more attention than the immediate and specific topics of the negotiation. They generally far

> I refer to this Asian approach to negotiation as holistic negotiating.

exceed and transcend the list of fixed value items found in U.S. distributive or integrative negotiating agendas.

In this manner, Asian negotiating is more holistic and comprehensive in nature and greatly differs from the singular focus on one's own interests or integrating and ceding new value items to the other party common in negotiating in America. Given these distinct characteristics and far-reaching factors, I refer to this Asian approach to negotiation as *holistic negotiating* and represent it visually in the following image.

Figure 1: Approach to Value in Asian and American Negotiating

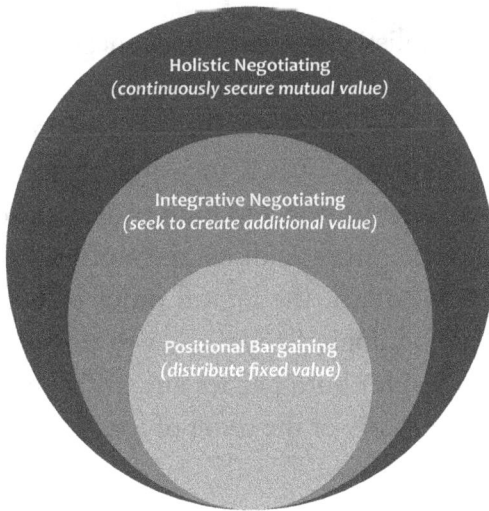

Holistic Negotiating
(continuously secure mutual value)

Integrative Negotiating
(seek to create additional value)

Positional Bargaining
(distribute fixed value)

Source: Robert Charles Azar

III. DIFFERENT TYPES OF LOGICS IN NEGOTIATING

A. LINEAR VS. HOLISTIC NEGOTIATING

Since in American negotiating companies focus on the needs of their own company and advocate for them, American negotiators generally list their items of interests and determine the most logical and beneficial order in which to pursue them in the negotiation. With their corporate interests listed in the most rational and advantageous manner possible, American negotiators pursue them in linear fashion, moving from one item to the next down the list. Agreement to one item helps move the negotiation forward, presumably offering a better position from which to win upcoming points. As these subsequent points are often based on the preceding items, an inability to come to agreement on a topic can result in the negotiations slowing down or becoming derailed. In addition, progress in the negotiation can be easily measured by how many of the topics of the negotiation have been agreed upon.

With their holistic approach, Asian negotiators, in contrast, commonly move from one topic to another in the negotiation, often without the logical order that American executives are accustomed to following. When focusing on the broader interests of the mutual relationship and joint project in addition to the immediate negotiating topics, discussions often cover items in a fashion that seems to lack the logical order of U.S. negotiators. The differing methodological approaches to the same negotiation can cause frustration for both parties due to the differing number of topics, the incongruity of the order of topics discussed, and the differing outcome focus.

With the priority given to relationship, mutual interest, and holistic logic in negotiations, being accommodating and adaptable is more important when negotiating in Asia than in the West. Contributing to this is the differing decision-making dynamics that Asian and American negotiators bring to the table. In addition to negotiating, U.S. decision-making is likewise conducted in what is considered to be a logical manner. Referred to as "rational decision-making," it calls for decisions to be made based on what is in the best interests of the company's bottom line seen from a rational perspective—the numbers need to justify the decision.

With this focus, American decision-making strives to select the best of the available options for each item, one at a time and in sequential order. An option is either better or worse. Favorable or unfavorable. Desirable or undesirable. Yes or no. Decisions are often made in that rational, binary fashion. Understandably, this dynamic does not leave much room for being accommodating or adaptable.

Meanwhile, the holistic approach that drives Asian negotiating likewise underpins decision-making there. As opposed to considering individual items one at a time, viewing and deciding based on selecting the best option for the entire project at-large in a holistic framework (and for the best interests of the mutual relationship of the parties) necessarily requires companies to be accommodating and adaptable. This dynamic profoundly impacts the degree of compromise in Asian negotiations, which is discussed in chapter two.

These two greatly differing approaches are ever-present in East-West negotiations. At a minimum, they are a source of continual frustration and misunderstanding. They make it more difficult for U.S. executives to demonstrate the requisite commitment to the mutual interests of the business project and for Asian executives to develop the required comfort level in the area of relationship building. While winning agreement from Asian companies to individual items on the list of negotiating priorities may be tactical wins during the course of a negotiation for a U.S. firm, such wins may in the end result in strategic losses. In the worst-

> While winning agreement to individual items may be a tactical win, it may result in strategic loss.

case scenario, these differences often cause negotiations to fall apart. Western executives need to be aware of these fundamentally different and ever-present undercurrents when negotiating in Asian markets.

B. CONTRACTUAL OBLIGATION VS. RELATIONAL OBLIGATION

Another result of this holistic negotiating dynamic is that Asian companies do not specify the responsibilities of each party in the detail that Americans do. Of course, roles and general areas of responsibility are discussed and agreed upon, but they typically are not delineated with the degree of detail and specificity that American executives are accustomed to having in business agreements. There are two reasons for this.

First, realizing that the challenges any business project faces will, quite naturally, change over time as market and competitive conditions evolve, the Asian approach focuses on the needs of and mutual commitment to the total project instead of on the individual company and its tasks. This results in negotiated agreements being much more fluid in Asia than in America as will be analyzed in the next chapter.

Second, as a result of both parties being committed to their mutual relationship, it is expected that all parties will act in good faith to engage in tasks that become required over time to meet each new challenge and to continue to advance the success of the project, regardless of what the previously executed business agreement may or may not say about it.

Whereas American negotiations and business focus on specific roles, responsibilities, and tasks of the companies involved, the Asian focus is on commitment to the long-term success of the business project itself as well as the mutual relationship. Consequently, the American business agreement excels in making sure that the participants engage in the specific roles and tasks delineated in it. The Asian approach excels in making sure each participant is committed to performing the changing roles and tasks the joint project requires over time. The Asian approach affords the companies involved greater flexibility to meet the needs of the project as those needs evolve over the long term. The American approach less so.

The American approach locks each company into specified roles and tasks they are contractually obligated to provide as delineated in the business agreement. At the same time, it gives the company a way to avoid engaging in any additional tasks not included in the agreement. An American company can decline any requests to engage in any roles or tasks it did not specifically agree to in the negotiated business agreement. This can be a valuable safeguard in the event a business partner makes requests the U.S. company is not interested in or the project is not going well and the company wishes to cut its losses and exit.

In contrast, while not bearing the same level of contractual focus on specific tasks as American companies, Asian companies are committed to carrying out project tasks that can be reasonably expected of them over time because they are committed to the long-term success of the joint venture as well as to the underlying mutual relationship of the parties involved. Through their relationships and business agreements, Asian companies are on the hook for a lot more than American companies are.

In summary, while the American approach to negotiating and conducting business puts companies in a position to be *contractually* obligated, the Asian approach makes companies *relationally* obligated. That is, Asian companies are obligated to act due to the expectations of the relationship as well as the joint project.

> While the American approach to negotiating puts companies in a position to be *contractually* obligated, the Asian approach makes companies *relationally* obligated.

Because they are obligated to much more than American firms, being relationally obligated to a joint business project for the long term reinforces even further the Asian preference for wanting to establish a sufficient comfort level and strong relationship before they decide to do business with a new business partner. We again see why it is imperative for American executives to understand and appropriately factor in the importance of relationship when negotiating with Asian firms.

From the Asian perspective, the importance of building that favorable working relationship has practical value. Namely, that the favorable working relationship will outlive individual business projects. Since Asian companies often maintain the relationship even after the business venture itself has concluded, it is very easy to start subsequent projects together as the relationship is already in place. When a company needs to secure a partner for a new project, it is much more likely to approach a company with whom it already has a relationship than with a company it does not.

As a result of these factors, negotiating in Asia requires more time than in other geographic areas. These factors also contribute to why Asian companies are slow to sign a business agreement, given the greater degree of obligation they are taking on.

IV. VARYING TIME PERSPECTIVES

Another difference in the way Americans and Asians approach negotiating and engage in business is that while Americans are more oriented toward the short term, Asians generally employ a long-term perspective.

This is critically important as Asian executives need to see that the American company they are negotiating with is likewise committed to working together for the long term and is willing to make decisions based on what

> While Americans are more oriented toward the short term, Asians generally employ a long-term perspective.

is in the long-term—not just short-term—interests of the project. This can entail making short-term sacrifices for the sake of the long-term interests of the joint business. A common area this is seen in is how profit and investment are prioritized.

For example, U.S. companies generally seek to maximize profit as quickly as possible in a new project. Management plans for and executes business to maximize profits for the short term. Likewise, Wall Street evaluates the profit performance of U.S. companies and their management in short-term intervals—on a quarterly basis.

By contrast, Asian firms often seek to invest more upfront to maximize the project's launch and gain market share for long-term profitability, even though that usually means smaller profit in the short term. Why is this so? Long-term profit stability is viewed as providing long-term stability for the company and for its business interests.

In order to meet short term profit and stock price targets, American firms frequently and quite matter-of-factly engage in numerous corporate actions including the following:

- Employee layoffs

- Reduction or cancellation of investment in plant, equipment, research and development, employee training, expansion, and new product launches

- Asset liquidation

Asian executives are amazed at these practices of management in the U.S., especially how employees are laid off when it seems a recession may be looming in the future. Workers are laid off even before the recession has started, so that layoffs to prepare for an apparent recession may actually hasten or even contribute to the start of a recession. In short, this practice of cutting costs to protect profit for the short term in response to the possibility of a recession not yet started is often perceived as a self-fulfilling prophecy.

This practice is alien to most companies in Asia where, as discussed later in this chapter, companies have a social obligation to contribute to the well-being of society at large, including by providing stable employment for workers. Furthermore, this short-term perspective is viewed negatively as being short-sighted because it does not value the assets of the company (especially employees) and is detrimental to the long-term interests, market share, and stability of a business.

This difference between short-term and long-term perspectives results in significantly different strategic objectives, investment priorities, and resource allocation. Furthermore, these differing perspectives can be a constant source of disagreement and friction when negotiating and conducting business with Asian companies. I have witnessed time and again how disagreement over these perspectives and priorities caused both the negotiations as well as joint business projects to break down. In short, differing time perspectives between America and Asia can be a major fault line when negotiating in Asian markets.

> Differing time perspectives between America and Asia can be a major fault line when negotiating in Asian markets.

American companies are known for not hesitating to discontinue a business venture if it does not meet short-term goals. While the "cut your losses" approach to business commonplace in the States makes sense from the perspective of rational decision-making, it does not translate well into the way business is conducted in Asian markets. How should U.S. executives deal with this gulf between their short-term perspective and the Asian long-term approach?

During negotiations, American executives need to demonstrate to Asian executives that they too are taking a long-term view of the joint business and are willing to bring to the project the requisite investment of people, equipment, and capital for the long term. Without this, the Asian company often finds it difficult to form a sufficient comfort level to negotiate or work together. If they do proceed without this comfort level, they relegate secondary priority to your business project. To maximize success in international markets, you need your overseas partners to engage in your business with priority focus. This is another example of how not effectively navigating the culture-based differences in business practices precludes American firms from achieving optimal success in Asian markets.

This concern is especially true regarding small- and medium-sized American companies as they typically do not have the same resources and staying power as large corporations do to stick it out if sales turn out to be slower than initially expected. One Japanese executive expressed this to me in this way: "The graveyard of foreign companies in Japan is very crowded. We Japanese are not eager to be a part of that." A traditional Japanese proverb expresses their longer time perspective as "enduring on top of a stone for three years" (*ishi no ue mo san nen* 石の上も三年).

While a long-term perspective is common throughout Asia, the degree of its significance there is not uniform. Specifically, the long-term approach to business is practiced to varying degrees throughout the region. In particular, Korea is on the opposite end of the timeline. In looking at Far East markets, a long-term approach is more prevalent in China and Japan than in Korea. Korea engages in negotiating with an approach that can be even shorter than what is typical in America. This is illustrated below in Figure 2.

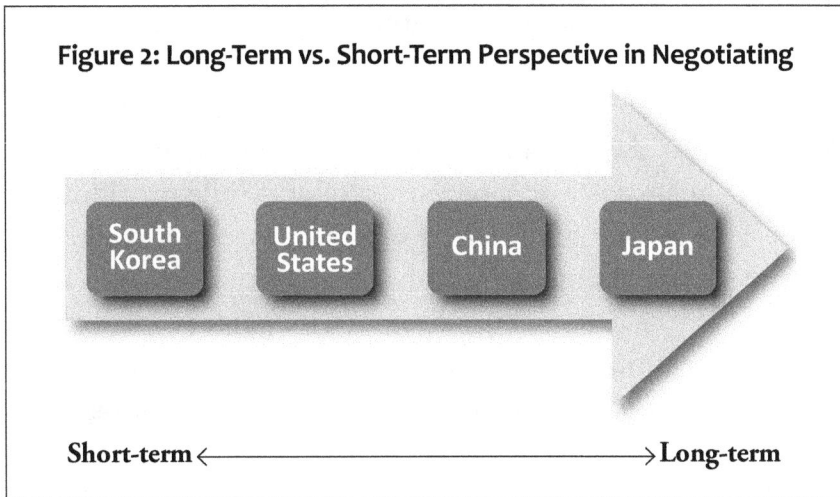

Figure 2: Long-Term vs. Short-Term Perspective in Negotiating

Short-term ⟵──────────────────────⟶ Long-term

Source: Robert Charles Azar

V. IMPACT OF SOCIETAL OBLIGATIONS

The over-riding focus of management in American firms is corporate profitability. Companies are free to singularly pursue their bottom line. Regarding corporate social responsibility, they are free to elect if, when, and to what degree they contribute to society. When they do contribute, it typically takes the form of contributing to specific organizations or activities in society, e.g., supporting the arts, an education program, a sports team, or a sports arena.

In recent years, a greater number of American companies are electing to focus on the "triple bottom line"—that is, the company's stakeholders, society at large, and the environment. This includes major Fortune 500 companies as well as B Corps. However, making contributions to societal activities on an elective basis and even the triple bottom line focus are nowhere near the same as societal obligations that firms face in many Asian markets.

Generally speaking, Asian businesses are expected to contribute to the benefit of society at large. They do so first through the product or service they offer. While providing its product or service for profit is certainly part of a company's motivation, providing their product or service is also seen as an act to benefit society at large. Second, companies contribute to society by maintaining stable employment. Third, firms view their activities as advancing their country's well-being. This is part of their *raison d' etre* as well as their corporate social responsibility.

Social considerations in Asia often preclude options that a company might otherwise wish to select—options that may be available to American firms not under the aegis of such responsibilities. The greatest example of how societal obligations can limit management options is seen in how they prevent companies from easily laying off employees to meet profit goals or eliminate redundancies created by entering into joint business projects with other firms, as is commonly done in the States.

Just how much stronger is this broader notion of societal obligation in Asia? In citing an example from Japan, Matsushita Konosuke, the founder and CEO of the Panasonic Corporation (formerly known as Matsushita Electric Co.), explained the social obligation of Japanese management and companies to employees and society at large as follows:

If the result of hard work is not black ink, and if it does not contribute to the prosperity of the country and the society nor to the enhancement of the standards of living of our employees, Matsushita Electric has no reason to exist. If it has no reason for existence, we should dissolve Matsushita Electric — **PHP Institute, Inc.,** ***Matsushita Konosuke: His Life & Legacy*** **(Tokyo: PHP Institute, Inc., 1994), pp.34-35.**

Inamori Kazuo is founder and CEO of the Kyocera Corporation, one of Japan's most successful Fortune 50 companies and is regarded as the most prominent business leader in present day Japan. He echoed the words of Matsushita when he wrote:

The pursuit of profit is the driving force behind business as well as many other human endeavors, and there is thus nothing wrong with wanting to make money. We should not pursue profit, however, for the benefit of ourselves alone. We need to "greedily" desire what is best for others and strive to promote the common [societal] good. If we do so, we too will benefit and the scope of our profit will greatly expand in the process.

Running a company, for example, is in itself a service to others and to society. — **Inamori Kazuo,** ***A Compass to Fulfillment: Passion and Spirituality in Life and Business*** **(New York: McGraw Hill, 2010), page 82.**

Commenting on an enterprise's social responsibility not

to lay off employees, Morita Akio, the co-founder and President of the Sony Corporation stated:

> *I discovered very quickly that in Western countries, employers would get rid of some personnel when a recession seemed imminent. It was a shock to me, because in Japan we never do this, unless we are completely desperate. If the [company's] administration takes the risk and responsibility of hiring personnel, then it also assumes responsibility for giving them work. It's not the employee who is responsible for this agreement. Also, when there is a recession, why should the personnel suffer because of a decision made by the administration who gave them a job?*
>
> — **http://www.quoteswise.com/akio-morita-quotes-2.html**

Strong societal obligation is a factor that is ever-present in the negotiating room with Asian executives and can have a direct or indirect influence on negotiating options, choices, and outcomes. They must consider not only how their negotiating decisions will impact their company but also their corporate social responsibilities. At the top of that list of responsibilities is stable employment and the firm's long-term viability. Management in Asia is often viewed as being more conservative than the States. Corporate social responsibility considerations are one reason why.

In some Asian nations, companies also have the additional societal obligation to directly contribute to their government's national economic development objectives. Let's look at Korea. The country's four major conglomerates—known as *chaebol* (재벌) in Korean—together are responsible for as much as eighty percent of the country's economy and, given their scale, have a far-reaching impact on the entire nation's economy and well-being. These companies have little choice but to factor the economic development goals and objectives of their government into management decisions. One of Samsung's mottos succinctly states this nation-benefiting social obligation: "We do business for the sake of nation building!"

> Societal obligations play a much more significant role in Asian business decisions than in the States.

The social obligation to contribute to their government's economic directions is especially pronounced in Asian countries with state run economies such as China and Vietnam. In those markets, many of the largest companies are state owned and run and are obliged to follow the ten-year economic development plans that their country's government issues every decade. In short, societal obligations play a much more significant role in Asian business decisions than in the States, and American executives need to be cognizant of this factor when negotiating and proposing options in those markets.

VI. CONFLICTING TIME PERIODS AND PACES

It is noteworthy that not only are the time perspectives used when negotiating and conducting business different as discussed above but the very definition of time periods such as short term, midterm, and long term are significantly different in America and Asia.

China employs the longest time horizons. It is not uncommon for large Chinese corporations to work with business plans that go out five or even ten years since, as we noted above, having embarked on its move to industrialize, China's central government follows ten-year plans for developing and managing the nation's industry and economy. Companies by necessity then also follow business plans that cover multiple years.

In addition to the business reasons given above for Asia's long-term outlook, there are cultural roots for it as well. Namely, Asia's long-term outlook is in part the result of Asian nations having significantly longer histories than America: 6,000 years for China, 4,000 years for Korea, and 2,000 years for Japan. Quite a contrast to our two-hundred-and forty-two-year history! With this historical context in mind, I was able to appreciate how, when discussing time horizons in China and Taiwan, I have often been told by executives that "for Chinese, long term is measured not in years but in generations"!

In Korea, however, it is noteworthy that while this longer time horizon applies to large corporations, small- and middle-sized companies are quite a different story. They are at the other end of the time horizon spectrum. They constantly seek to accelerate the pace of business and want everything to move quickly—whether it is negotiating, planning, launching the business, or turning a profit. Executives there do everything they can to hasten the pace.

The Korean phrase commonly used for this accelerated pace is *ppalli ppalli* (빨리빨리), literally meaning "quickly, quickly." It represents the fast pace and short-term outlook that is prevalent in much of that market. *Ppalli ppalli* is comparable in nuance to the American phrase "get it done *yesterday*." Rushing matters is a cultural dynamic at play in both negotiating and business in general throughout this sector of the Korean market.

Let's look at an example of this *ppalli ppalli* dynamic encountered in the Korean market. My initial meeting with potential business partners there would usually include a presentation to them on the background of my American or European client company, the products they wanted to sell in Korea, the strategy behind the marketing plan for the Korean market, and how Korea fits into the client's global business strategy. When I would be only forty or fifty percent of the way through the initial presentation, it was common for a senior Korean executive to stop me and say, "Thank you for the presentation. We definitely want to sell those products in Korea. Let's sign your sales agreement now." I would invariably reply, "But I haven't finished the presentation. You have not yet heard everything about the company, its product, and strategic goals." Their response generally went along the lines of "That's ok. We can see this is a big opportunity, and we want it. Let's get started *very quickly*!" Quick to negotiate. Quick to decide. Quick to start.

While this fast-paced negotiating and decision-making in Korea can seem refreshing to American companies after the often painfully slow pace of negotiations in other Asian markets, it contains huge risks. Negative consequences of this short term, rush approach are that details are overlooked, items can fall through the cracks, and projects can get executed without sufficient preparation. U.S. executives need to be aware of this dynamic and the dangers it presents.

> In short, Korean companies can be fast on but also fast off.

Another risk is that your business partner in the Korean market can walk away from your business just as quickly as they got on board. In short, Korean companies can be fast on but also fast off. Given this dynamic, American executives should not be surprised when commitments made in negotiations end up being short-lived. There have been numerous occasions where I was retained by American and European clients to salvage their business operations in Korea because their local partner there abruptly withdrew from it.

Japan lies in between China and Korea in terms of time horizons. In contrast to Korea where both the negotiations and the business project itself can conclude quickly, in Japan and China the negotiations are longer but so is the collaboration; the courtship is long but so is the resulting marriage.

This is especially true in Japan where relationships and the commitments made in them are taken extremely seriously and, as pointed out earlier, are expected to outlast the business project being negotiated. This important consideration is discussed in greater detail in chapter two.

Figure 3 provides a representative comparison of the differing paces of negotiations among America, China, Japan, and Korea.

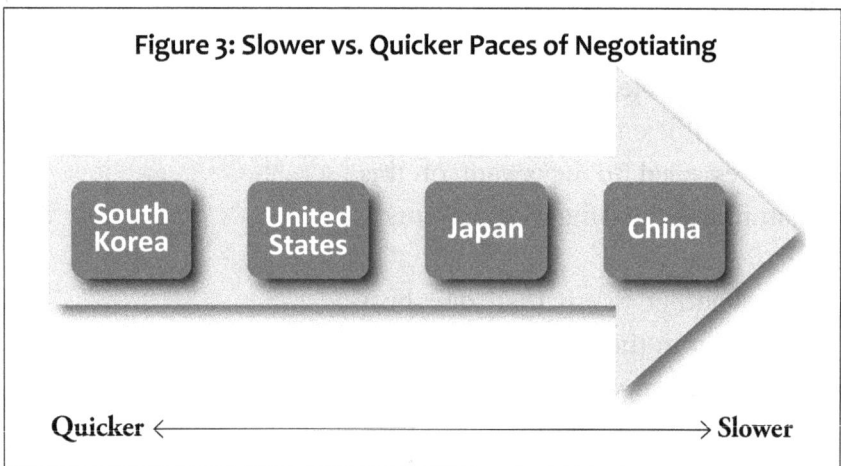

Figure 3: Slower vs. Quicker Paces of Negotiating

South Korea   United States   Japan   China

Quicker ⟵   ⟶ Slower

Source: Robert Charles Azar

INSIGHTS

Clearly, American and Asian approaches to negotiating vary significantly. Some of the numerous examples we explored include the following dozen factors:

1. The level of consideration given to the other parties' interests
2. The degree to which negotiating is a zero-sum game versus a win-win proposition
3. The role and consequences of relationship
4. The number of value items negotiated
5. The degree and timing of when bottom line positions are revealed
6. How bottom line positions are revealed
7. The different types of logic executives use in steering negotiations
8. What the parties to the negotiation are obligated to do
9. Varying time perspectives
10. The impact on negotiations of a company's societal obligations
11. Conflicting time periods
12. Differing paces of negotiations

CHAPTER 2

DYNAMICS GOVERNING

NEGOTIATING

I. CENTRALITY OF RELATIONSHIP

In comparing America and Asia, so many of the funda-mental differences in the practice of negotiating and the dynamics that underpin them stem from the central role played by rela-tionship. The numerous facets of Asian negotiating influenced by relationship include the following twenty items:

1. Approach to negotiating
2. Purpose of negotiating
3. Goals in negotiating
4. Dynamics governing negotiations
5. Degree of importance given to the other party's interests
6. Timing for presenting negotiation objectives

7. Method of presenting negotiating objectives
8. Protocols informing negotiations
9. Dealing with differences in bargaining positions
10. Depth of information requested and disclosed
11. Degree of compromising necessary
12. Decision-making in negotiations
13. Pace of negotiations
14. Communication dynamics informing negotiations
15. Length of negotiations
16. Recognizing and resolving conflict
17. Time horizons used in negotiations
18. Who participates in negotiating meetings
19. Seating arrangements in negotiating
20. Venue of negotiations

Given the prominence of relationship, it makes sense to begin our comparison of negotiating dynamics by discussing exactly what "relationship" means in Asia and how it impacts the negotiation process and outcome.

A.   DIVERGENT DEFINITIONS OF RELATIONSHIP

In U.S. business, when we say two companies have a relationship, it generally means, excluding any ownership ties, that the two companies have conducted business together—they have a track record. It is not necessary to have a relationship in order to commence negotiating or establish business collaboration. Accordingly, two companies conduct business together and a

> While collaboration precedes relationship in America, in Asia relationship precedes collaboration.

relationship follows. A relationship is the result of engaging in business together. In other words, in the U.S., business collaboration precedes relationship. Equally important, relationship is the result of collaboration in the American context.

> The meaning of relationship throughout Asia varies significantly in both nuance and substance from market to market.

This is quite different from relationship in Asian business. Actually, it is the exact opposite. Generally speaking, having a relationship is a prerequisite in order for companies to work together. Consequently, while collaboration precedes relationship in America, the opposite is true in Asia—relationship precedes collaboration. Furthermore, relationship enables the conducting of business together in Asia; relationship is not the result of collaboration as is the case in the U.S.

What does relationship mean in Asia? On its most basic level, relationship means having a comfort level and familiarity with the other party. That meaning is commonplace throughout most of Asia and serves as a good baseline definition. However, the meaning of relationship is not uniform throughout Asia. On the contrary, it varies significantly in both nuance and substance from market to market. Let's take a closer look at how the meaning of relationship varies among China, Japan, and Korea.

1. MEANING OF RELATIONSHIP IN CHINA

The word for "relationship" in the Chinese language is *quanxi* (关系), and its importance in that society is often spoken of. Interestingly, in China, *quanxi* connections are less a relationship of familiarity and friendship as is common throughout most of Asia and more fundamentally are bonds of mutual obligation to exchange favors with each other.

Relationships and their built-in obligation to exchange favors are developed over time by engaging in acts for the benefit of the other party. Each party engages in those acts for the purpose of generating good will, building a relationship to win the recipient's favor, and also to establish an indebtedness the receiving party then has an obligation to repay by returning favors to the other. In this manner, the two parties are tied together in a relationship of mutual obligation to reciprocate favors.

While Chinese companies certainly prefer to establish and maintain *quanxi* connections with those they know well and are friends with, that familiar and personal dimension is not a requirement. A *quanxi* connection is possible with a party that one can do favors for and cause to become indebted to you. In these cases, the relationships are less bonds of comfort level and familiarity between parties and are more utilitarian connections.

Why is the obligation to return favors so prominent in the meaning of relationship in China? The dynamic governing this aspect of *quanxi* connections is the traditional Chinese cultural value of reciprocity (*yi* 義). Reciprocity is one of the fundamental ethical principles of China's Confucian tradition that has governed Chinese society as well as many other Asian countries for centuries. It states that the returning of favors or acts of kindness is one of the paramount social values and obligations of all people. Failure to reciprocate favors would cause a person to lose face (one of the main social and ethical faux pas in all Confucian-based societies) and be deemed an untrustworthy person.

This obligation-oriented meaning of relationship in China is unique in Asia, where typically relationship involves a comfort level and personal familiarity between the parties. That is true despite the fact that it is based on the main teachings of traditional Confucianism. Confucius lived in the sixth to fifth centuries BC, and his teachings spread to Korea in the fourth century AD and to Japan in the fifth century AD, as well as throughout most of Asia Pacific where it has dominated Asian cultures ever since. Yet the Chinese view of relationship in business is not common in other Asian markets.

2.   MEANING OF RELATIONSHIP IN JAPAN

In Japan, the relationship between collaborating companies means significantly more than simply comfort level and familiarity. More fundamentally, relationship also includes trust. In fact, companies refer to their relationships with companies they collaborate with as a "trust relationship" (*shinrai kankei* 信頼関係), and it entails a *mutual commitment* to the other party's corporate interests *for the long term*. It is knowing and having full confidence that your business partner can be counted on to take into consideration your company's interests as well as their own as you work together. That applies both during the negotiating process and thereafter as well.

The meaning of the word trust in Japanese highlights and reinforces this central and essential meaning of relationship in Japanese negotiating and business. *Shin-rai* (trust) has two related meanings:

- To highly evaluate a person or thing

- To feel that one can entrust all matters to the care of the other party

As we can see, the notion that a trust relationship includes having confidence that your business partner can be counted on to take into consideration your company's interests as well as their own as you work together is deeply imbedded in Japanese culture. This is aptly expressed in the ubiquitous Japanese phrase *okagesama de* (お陰様で). Its literal meaning is "thanks to you" and is used to say "you're welcome." So, when the company your firm is working with expresses thanks to you for doing something for them or the mutual project, you reply "thanks to you" to indicate that you could do it because both parties are equally committed to their mutual relationship and interests. Western executives will find that this notion is strongly imbedded in Japan's way of negotiating and conducting business.

In Japan, one fundamental way companies show that they highly evaluate another party—the first meaning of trust in the definition above—is by demonstrating respect at all times. This is another reason why respect plays a such significant role in the dynamics of relationships as well as the communication between parties in business. This heightened role and impact of needing to demonstrate respect is covered in detail in chapter four of this book.

This second meaning of trust—that is, to feel that one can entrust all matters to the care of the other party—is another way we can see how central the idea of looking out for each other's interests is in Japanese business; it is a prerequisite to succeeding in both business negotiation and collaboration.

This integral nature of trust in business relationships in Japan is unique in Asia and markedly different from the States; in the latter, familiarity and trust are not prerequisites for commencing negotiations or business collaboration. This, of course, is not to say that trust and comfort level are not present in the negotiation process in the U.S. They certainly are. If a company lacks a comfort level or distrusts another company, they may hesitate to negotiate or initiate business collaboration, scale back their collaboration, or simply refrain from negotiating or working together. Trust factor differences between Asia and the U.S. are found in these three areas:

- The degree of importance of trust and comfort level

- How trust and comfort levels are established

- The far-reaching and long-term impact these factors have on business

In America, trust in negotiating and in business develops when a party demonstrates consistency between one's words and actions. As Harvard Business Essentials' book *Negotiating* explains:

> *Trust is created when people see tangible evidence that one's words and actions are in harmony. Therefore, avoid making commitments you may be unable to honor, and always do what you have committed to do.* — **Harvard Business Essentials, *Negotiating* (Cambridge, MA: Harvard Business Review Press, 2003) p. 118.**

It is generally true in most countries that parties create trust by demonstrating consistency between their statements and actions. It is important to note that this condition is met to a greater degree after the joint business project commences more than during the negotiating process.

> Trust is *transactional* in the American approach to negotiating and business. In contrast, in Japan, trust is *relational*.

Another point of distinction is that because trust is based on the parties demonstrating consistency in their transactions with each other, trust is transactional in the American approach to negotiating and business. In contrast, in Japan, since trust is an integral part of the relationship that is the foundation of all business collaboration, trust is relational. Trust develops based on the quality, length, and commitment in the relationship the parties establish between them. That involves many aspects beyond consistency between words and deeds. For example, we have discussed the need for both parties to demonstrate a long-term commitment to work for the mutual benefit for both parties and for the joint business. Other concrete aspects are discussed throughout this book.

It is clear that the threshold level of trust requisite for companies to successfully negotiate and conduct business together is significantly greater in Japan and other Asian markets than in America.

The major features of trust relationship in Japan include the following six major facets:

1. The parties' relationship will be based on the aim of advancing the mutual interests of all companies involved.
2. Commitment to the relationship is both mutual and, as much as possible, equal.
3. Decisions regarding the business will be made with appropriate consideration of each other's circumstances and objectives.
4. Both parties' commitment to their relationship is long term.
5. Both parties' commitment to their business project is long term.
6. The mutual relationship between companies is intended to last beyond any specific business project.

3.   MEANING OF RELATIONSHIP IN KOREA

Among the three nations of China, Japan, and Korea, relationship plays the least significant role in Korea. In that market, relationship generally means familiarity and comfort level, the common meaning of relationship throughout most of Asia.

However, unlike in Japan or China, having a relationship is not a prerequisite for commencing negotiations or a mutual business project. A quick self-introduction or introduction by a third party is sufficient for companies previously unknown to each other to enter into negotiations straightaway.

In addition, relationship does not include the meaning of being mutually committed to each other's business interests. Instead, each company focuses on pursuing its own interests while collaborating. When a joint business ceases to meet the

> Korean executives refer to those executives they have established a relationship with as *"i chin-gu"* "this friend."

short-term needs of a company, it is common to cease collaboration at that point. Both of these characteristics are much the same as in the States. Relationship does not act as a bond to keep the companies together. In this way, neither the threshold of relationship needed to work together nor the significance of relationship is as high in that market. In short, the role of relationship is not as central in Korea as it is in the rest of the Far East.

American firms can know that the Korean companies they are seeking to conduct business with have reached a sufficient level of familiarity and comfort with them when Korean executives refer to them as *"chin-gu"* (친구) when speaking in Korean. *Chin-gu* means "friend." Korean executives refer to those executives they have established a relationship with as *"i chin-gu"* (이친구)—"this friend." This is especially prevalent with small- and medium-sized Korean companies. In comparison, the term used in the Japanese market to refer to companies one has a trust relationship with is "partner" (パートナー). This is another indication of how the meaning of relationship as well as its degree of importance in Korean business is different and less significant in comparison to either Japan or China. Let's look further now at how the degree of importance given to relationship affects negotiating in Asia.

B. DIFFERING IMPORTANCE OF RELATIONSHIP IN NEGOTIATING

We have seen how the meaning of relationship in

negotiating and business is quite different between America and Asia. The degree of importance of relationship is likewise quite different, generally playing a greater role in Asia than the U.S. It is noteworthy, however, that its level of significance is not uniform in Asian markets.

In Japan, for example, the two aspects of relationship and the mutual business have equal significance. In many cases, Japanese companies consider the relationship to be even more important than the individual business project itself. This significantly impacts the decision-making of partner companies as it is not uncommon for companies to temper their decisions out of consideration of the interests of the mutual business project and its supporting relationship. This applies to the negotiating process as well.

This dynamic is not found in America where it is generally thought that business decisions should not be influenced by the relationship of the parties. It is often said that the mark of a professional is the ability to separate how they feel on a personal level from deciding the business matter at hand. Only decisions that are objective in that manner can be in the best interests of a firm's business.

Another factor supporting this American negotiating tendency is that, as discussed in chapter one, business in America is seen as being purpose driven; the project's aim is to achieve specified results. Accordingly, achieving the best result in negotiations and business projects is the primary focus, not relationship. In the final analysis, it is results that matter, not relationship.

As a consequence of these factors, U.S. companies generally do not give anywhere near the priority to relationship in negotiating that Asian entities do. Let's examine this more closely.

The seminal American book on negotiating *Getting to Yes: Negotiating Agreement Without Giving In* makes this point that giving priority importance to relationship should be avoided as it can be counterproductive in negotiations:

> *"However, any negotiation primarily concerned with the relationship runs the risk of producing a sloppy agreement."* — **Roger Fisher, William Ury and Bruce Patton, Getting To YES: Negotiating Agreement Without Giving In (New York: Penguin Books, 2011 third edition), p. 10.**

This U.S. view of relationship is aptly expressed in Harvard Business Essentials' book *Negotiation*. The section titled "Doing It Right" suggests that including relationship at all in negotiating the specifics of a deal can be detrimental:

> *"Negotiating expert Danny Ertel underscores the problems associated with negotiations in which elements of the deal and the relationship are intertwined:*
>
>> *'(Negotiators) fear that if they push too hard to get the best deal possible today, they may jeopardize their company's ability to do business with the other party in the future. Or they fear that if they pay too much attention to the relationship, they'll end up giving away too much and make a lousy deal. Though natural, such confusion is dangerous. It leaves the negotiator opened to manipulation by the other party.'*

"How can you avoid falling into this same trap? Ertel's advice is to distinguish between the deal and the relationship—that is, to draw a clear distinction between the components of the deal and the components of the relationship...." — **Harvard Business Essentials,** *Negotiating* **(Cambridge, MA: Harvard Business Review Press, 2003), pp. 115-116.**

How do you separate the deal from the relationship?

"Early in the negotiation is also the right time to focus on your relationship by separating it from the essence of what's being discussed in the negotiation. We call this negotiating on two tracks.... People often believe they need to make concessions or forgo their interests for the sake of the relationship.... Conceding like this in an attempt to make the other party happy is a mistake. You're not only giving away more than you should, you're also not improving the relationship itself, so you're not even getting what you think you are 'paying' for. Furthermore, you're probably making matters worse...." — **Jeff Weiss,** *HBR Guide to Negotiating* **(Cambridge, MA: Harvard Business Review Press, 2016), p.74-75.**

Not only is including relationship considerations in negotiating problematic for a *company's* efforts to gain the best results in negotiations but it is also dangerous for the *individual negotiators* themselves who engage in the negotiations:

"If relationships rank high among your organization's strategic goals, be forewarned that you could pay

a personal price in pursuing them. Why? Because many companies still talk out of both sides of their mouths. On the one hand, they say that long-term relationships matter. On the other hand, they generally reward negotiators for delivering on monetary or other measurable values: the most advantageous settlement, the lowest-cost supplier contract, the most favorable contract terms, and so on…. Negotiators must separate the deal from the broader relationship. — **Harvard Business Essentials, Negotiating (Cambridge, MA: Harvard Business Review Press, 2003), p. 118-119.**

Relationship in China is also very important but, in most cases, not to the same degree as in Japan where the relationship and project are equal. While relationship is ostensibly important in Korea as well, in practice it certainly is not as strong a causal or long-term factor in negotiating or conducting business as it is in China and Japan. The figure below depicts this difference in the degree of significance of relationship in negotiating and business in Asia.

Figure 4: Significance of Relationship in Negotiating and Business

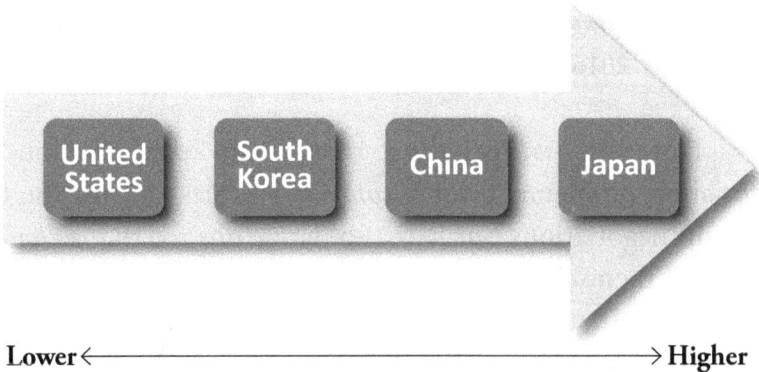

United States | South Korea | China | Japan

Lower ←——————————————→ Higher

Source: Robert Charles Azar

Just as the degree of significance of relationship in business differs in America and Asia, so too does the significance of relationship differ in the negotiating styles employed in these countries.

Figure 5 below illustrates the differing degree of relationship significance in distributive, integrative, and holistic negotiating.

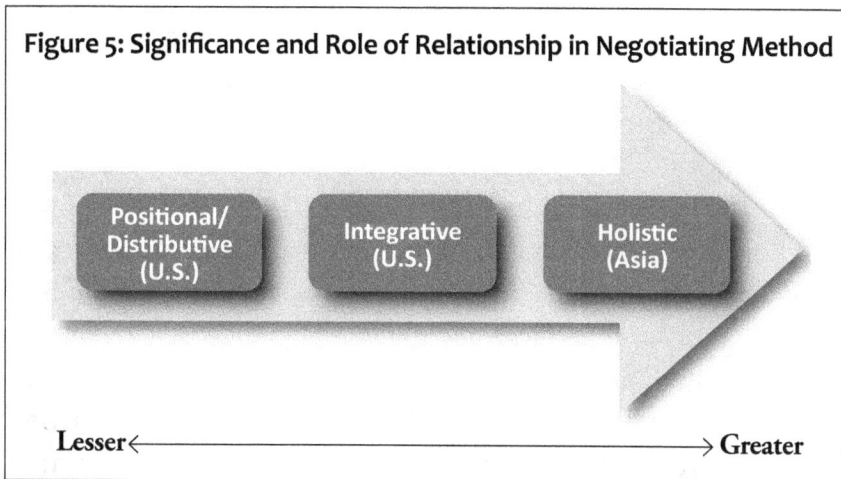

Figure 5: Significance and Role of Relationship in Negotiating Method

Positional/ Distributive (U.S.)

Integrative (U.S.)

Holistic (Asia)

Lesser ← ─────────────────── → Greater

Source: Robert Charles Azar

C. *INITIATING A BUSINESS RELATIONSHIP*

One might wonder if a relationship is necessary in order for companies to work together in Asia, how companies that do not have a relationship ever have the opportunity to do so. In these cases, a company can arrange to be introduced to the other company by a mutual third party having a pre-existing relationship with both companies. As long as the third party has a sufficient mutual relationship with the two companies, it will have both the ability and the comfort level to connect them through its introduction and, if required, involvement.

Third parties that commonly provide such introductions based on their mutual relationship with the two companies include:

- Companies such as banks, investment companies, business partners, consulting firms, or similar entities.

- Individuals who have a relationship with people in the two companies seeking to conduct business together.

The latter would include colleagues in the industry as well as fellow members of industry associations, school alumni, country clubs, sports groups, neighborhood associations, and the like.

While it is common in the States for alumni to utilize networks from their former colleges in a similar introduction manner, I was surprised to see how often the mutual connection is a former schoolmate from high school and even elementary school in Asian countries. It is common in Asia for former students to regularly attend alumni functions for secondary as well as post-secondary institutions over the course of their lives—another example of the importance of relationship and group identity in Asian markets.

> After companies that do not have a pre-existing relationship are introduced, they endeavor to build their relationship during the negotiation process.

After companies that do not have a pre-existing relationship are introduced, they endeavor to build their relationship during the negotiation process. This is done concurrently with discussing the business items of the negotiation. As mentioned in chapter one, developing a relationship and discussing the terms of the business need to be done simultaneously. If not, progress cannot be made in the negotiations.

D. *MAINTAINING YOUR BUSINESS RELATIONSHIPS*

As previously detailed, relationship is necessary for a company to decide to work with another company and, once started, the relationship supports the business project over the long term—business is relationship driven. As a result, building and managing that relationship must remain an on-going priority for a foreign company negotiating and engaging in business in Asia. The following twelve practical steps will help American executives maximize their success in relationship building and relationship management with their Asian partners:

1. Keep up close communication with your Asian partner on a regular basis, including face-to-face meetings several times a year
2. Provide a safe harbor environment within which Asian executives feel comfortable to discuss in a thorough and timely fashion challenges that arise in the joint business and mutual relationship
3. Be proactive in identifying challenges your Asian partner confronts in promoting your business and offer your assistance for best resolving them
4. Articulate and demonstrate that your company's commitment to the Asian company and market is long term

5. Provide the partner with advance notice of developments that are related to the joint project
6. Celebrate with your Asian partner milestone achievements in the mutual business
7. Congratulate your Asian partner on their major business successes that are unrelated to your joint project
8. Update your partner on new developments and breakthroughs at your company, even those unrelated to the joint business
9. Make opportunities for spending time together outside of official meetings by enjoying meals, after-hour drinks, golf, weekend activities, and industry events
10. Express appreciation for the opportunity to work together with your Asian partner, including gifts for their executives
11. Send New Year's greetings within the first three business days of each year
12. Remain polite, professional, timely, and dependable at all times, in all ways, in all matters, even with things that seem trivial from an American perspective

II. COMPROMISE, CONCESSIONS, AND BARGAINING

A. THE SIGNIFICANCE OF COMPROMISE, CONCESSIONS, AND BARGAINING

With this long-term, relationship-oriented approach to negotiating in Asia, it is expected that both parties will be favorably inclined to make compromises and concessions. As explained in chapter one, Asian negotiators generally do not utilize a zero-sum game approach or other techniques that force the other party into agreement. Instead they want to see that you are genuinely interested in the mutual benefit of both parties—not just in your own company's best interest—and your willingness to compromise is one concrete way this is demonstrated.

This negotiating dynamic is most prevalent in the Japanese market where compromise is viewed as being an essential part of establishing a "trust relationship." Remember, a trust relationship has at its core the commitment to the mutual interest of both companies as well as their joint business. The act of not compromising violates this fundamental commitment and prevents trust from developing.

> The act of not compromising violates this fundamental commitment and prevents trust from developing.

In the practice of Japanese negotiating, a company that will not compromise lacks "sincerity" (not negotiating in good faith in American cultural terms) and is not committed to trying to accommodate the interests of the other party and their mutual business. Such a company disqualifies itself as a viable partner. As we can see, trust being precluded in Japan due to unwillingness to compromise is quite different from trust being prevented in America due to inconsistency between word and action as discussed earlier.

In addition, as each company is expected to be guided by the mutual interests of both companies and their joint project, padding one's positions and haggling are not viewed favorably in

> Chinese typically pad their starting positions, sometimes to a degree greater than Americans do.

Japan. This can be another disqualifier in Japanese negotiations. As a result, bargaining is not significantly engaged in.

Compromise and concessions are expected in China. However, in contrast to Japan, haggling is a commonly used bargaining tool. As a result, unlike Japanese negotiators, Chinese typically pad their starting positions, sometimes to a degree greater than Americans do.

In Chinese negotiations, compromises and concessions are often used as leverage to win agreement to what a company considers its most important items. Chinese negotiators typically agree at the same time to several of an American company's points the Chinese have attached lower priority to in order to win agreement to their own priority items.

Further along this line, in the U.S., compromises, concessions, and bargaining are seen as one-for-one swaps—I agree to that term you are proposing and in exchange you agree to the item I am seeking. In China, compromises, concessions, and bargaining are not one-for-one exchanges. Rather they are negotiating tools whereby several lower priority items are bundled and given away together in order to gain high priority items.

This usually happens at the final stage of the negotiation. It is common for negotiations to drag on for an extended period with little apparent progress and then in the last phase, Chinese companies will suddenly agree to compromises and concessions to several items at once, often surprising Western negotiators. This is another example of how progress in negotiations takes longer there and may not proceed in the logical order American negotiators are accustomed to. It is important for U.S. executives to keep this dynamic in mind and not become discouraged when protracted negotiations seem to have accomplished little. When the negotiation reaches a critical mass stage for Chinese negotiators—that is, when they arrive at the point where they are ready to give a decision on several topics all at once—the negotiation will be catapulted into the next stage.

> When the negotiation reaches a critical mass stage for Chinese negotiators, the negotiation will be catapulted into the next stage.

From these positions, you can see Americans and Asians engage in compromises and concessions at different stages in the negotiations as well as for different reasons. This relates to chapter one's discussion of how Americans and Asians utilize a different type of logic in negotiating.

> Americans and Asians engage in compromises and concessions at different stages in the negotiations as well as for different reasons.

You will recall, U.S. companies engage linear logic in which the topics to be negotiated follow a rational order; topics are discussed one at a time in a sequential order so that subsequent decisions build on agreement to previous ones. As a result, it is natural that American negotiators seek compromises to items as they are needed throughout the course of the negotiations so the negotiations can progress.

Asian companies, in contrast, employ a holistic logic, viewing all topics as organically interconnected; rather than being addressed sequentially as in the States, topics are often bundled together and viewed in a comprehensive manner. The order of the topics in the negotiation can lack rational order from a Western perspective and some of the topics in each bundle of issues may seem unrelated to the immediate item being discussed. Since it is only in later stages of a negotiation that the complete picture of what is being negotiated comes into focus, Asian executives are often more comfortable putting off concessions throughout the earlier stages of the negotiations and then making several in the final phase of the process. As noted, in the case of China, this dynamic is also utilized as a negotiating tool to cede lower priority items in order to win high priority items.

> For Korean negotiators, it is fully expected that both parties will make compromises and concessions.

Finally, let's look at compromise, concessions, and bargaining in the Korean market. As noted earlier in this chapter, companies in Korea that have attained relationship status are viewed and referred to as friend (*chingu*). Friends are considered those who understand and are sympathetic to your situation, who naturally want to assist you. Therefore, for Korean negotiators, it is fully expected that both parties will make compromises and concessions. In one instance where the vice president of my client company asked his Korean counterpart over evening drinks why he agreed to so many of the American company's requests, the Korean executive replied very simply, "We are friends." This dynamic is especially common with small- and medium-sized enterprises in the Korean market.

As in China, Korean companies engage in posturing to a much greater degree than Japanese, including padding one's negotiating positions. In addition, Korean negotiators are quite passionate and persistent hagglers. In contrast to the relatively staid negotiating common in Japan and China, Korean negotiators often engage in haggling and bargaining with a boisterousness and forcefulness that belies the traditional name the Korean people affectionately use referring to their homeland—"The Land of the Morning Calm" (*cho-sun* 조선). A negotiator raising his voice, appearing to be upset, or engaging in an emotional outburst is viewed negatively in China and Japan. Not so in Korea.

> In Asia, to compromise in negotiating is generally not seen as a weakness but rather a strength.

In Asia, to compromise in negotiating is generally not seen as a weakness but rather a strength. Compromising is a strong indication that your relationship with the other company is a priority to you—literally, you are willing to put your money where your mouth is. Accordingly, compromise is an important way in which American executives can demonstrate to Asian executives that your relationship with them is important to your company as well.

> While in distributive negotiating, parties add new value items *during the negotiation*, negotiating in Asia requires companies to prepare value items *before the start of the negotiation.*

With this in mind, it is advisable to start negotiations with several "give away" items that you have prepared in advance that are likely to be of interest to the other party. Consequently, as discussed in the previous chapter, while in the distributive negotiating method common in the U.S., the parties seek to add new value items *during the negotiation* that the other party can "win," in contrast, negotiating in Asia requires companies to prepare value items *before the start* of the negotiation.

The Asian negotiating dynamic of compromising, together with its commitment to the mutual relationship and the long-term success of the project, often causes foreign executives to feel bewildered. Just how much do you need to compromise during negotiations? It is not necessary to compromise on or agree to every proposal put forth. Give and take is expected from both sides, and both parties must be comfortable with compromises made if the agreement is to be viable and have longevity.

So then what degree of flexibility and compromise should American executives demonstrate when negotiating in order to demonstrate "sincerity" and not alienate their Asian counterparts? There is no hard and fast rule. It will vary from industry to industry, company to company, and situation to situation. As a general guideline, I have found that the degree of flexibility that is expected rises the more important the matter is. In the end, striking a sensible balance between the needs of the project and the realities of your company is always a reasonable—and sustainable—approach. This can only be decided on a case-by-case basis. When it is not possible to compromise or agree to a concession, American executives will be well-served to carefully explain the reasons why your firm cannot. While not required in the States, doing so in Asia goes a long way toward enabling your counterparts not to react negatively to your decision or view it as a hinderance to building your mutual relationship. This is further discussed in the next section.

B.   AVOIDING COMPROMISE

Given the importance in Asia of compromises both during the negotiations and even after the project begins, the issue becomes how can American companies avoid agreeing to a request for a compromise without alienating Asian partners. The "we are not contractually obligated to do that" response that is commonplace in the States is counterproductive in Asia and should be avoided. It makes your company come across as inflexible and, rather than thinking about the needs of the mutual project, focused only on your company. Simply put, the notion of "not being contractually obligated" does not translate well culturally and, more importantly, relationally in Asia. Being a good business partner, having a good relationship, is defined in part by giving priority to the mutual needs of the project as well as one's own needs. Hence the need to compromise is notably greater in negotiating in Asia than in the States.

During the course of most negotiations, it is common for items to arise that are not possible for your company to compromise on. In that case, endeavor as well as you can to provide your reason(s) in a way that translates well culturally.

> The notion of "not being contractually obligated" does not translate well culturally and, more importantly, relationally in Asia.

This is an example of how a cultural facilitator plays a crucial role in negotiating in Asia, as discussed in detail in chapter five. In addition, when unable to compromise, it can be helpful to offer a concession on another item instead, even an unrelated item. This is another reason why commencing negotiations in Asia already having prepared "give away" items is highly recommended.

What other practical steps beside "give away" items can American executives take to avoid agreeing to unwanted requests or proposals from Asian partners both during the negotiations and once the project has begun? I have found that the following negotiating tactics work well:

- If applicable, you could take the position that a proposal goes against the established corporate policies of your company. Asians respect that and realize nothing can be done about it. This reason translates well culturally and usually lays that proposal to rest.

- You could reply by saying that your company has thought about that option before but never came to a decision about it. Offer that the matter can be discussed further in your company. This is an effective way of deflecting the issue while demonstrating flexibility in the negotiation.

- You could respond by saying that your company has never considered that before but will look into it. When all else fails, this catchall reply is generally favorably received. As discussed later in this chapter, decision-making in companies in Asia generally includes all the departments affected by a proposal and, consequently, takes a considerable amount of time. If you reply to Asian counterparts with this response, you loudly signal that a lengthy amount of time will be required for your company to examine the proposal and be in a position to respond to it.

- Once the project has begun, you could reply to additional proposals and requests by taking the position that in America the terms of an agreement are not changed once the project begins. However, given the importance of your mutual relationship, you might want to respond by stating that you will discuss with your fellow executives if it is possible to explore this matter *as a special case*. This allows you to signal that acquiescence is not likely but that your company values and respects its relationship with your Asian partner. It also establishes that future requests from the Asian company are not likely to be well received by your company.

C. DEGREES OF COMPROMISE NECESSARY

How does the degree of compromise in Asian negotiating compare with the U.S.? In America, the goal of winning one's desired terms is given greater importance than relationship. It is for that reason that the book *Getting to Yes: Negotiating Agreement Without Giving In* admonishes against compromise for the sake of the mutual relationship: "Our point is that you should not give in for the purpose of trying to improve a relationship" (p. 161). The book's subtitle likewise highlights that notion—*Negotiating Agreement Without Giving In*.

In its *HBR Guide to Negotiating*, Harvard Business Review comments on this American distributive negotiating practice by advising that negotiators should avoid:

> *...sacrificing your interests in order to preserve the relationship. Deal with the relationship*

separately. — **Jeff Weiss,** *HBR Guide to Negotiating* **(Cambridge, MA: Harvard Business Review Press, 2016), p. 101.**

This advice is given in the book's section entitled "Watch Out for Common Mistakes." This dynamic is applicable for negotiating in America, but as this chapter has demonstrated, it is not advisable to separate corporate interest and relationship when negotiating in Asia.

Likewise, Harvard's *Negotiation* sums up the common U.S. view of compromise in the context of promoting relationship as follows:

"The best advice about concessions is to avoid the impulse to make them....Remember, too, that deal making isn't about making friends." — **Harvard Business Essentials,** *Negotiating* **(Cambridge, MA: Harvard Business Review Press, 2003), p. 54.**

As we have seen in this chapter, the degree of compromise necessary in negotiating is greater in Asia than America.

It is critically important to realize that while relationship may imply friendship and a history of working together in the States, the meaning is totally different in Asia. What is meant by relationship is so much broader, more fundamental, and consequential than simply having a friendly rapport or a record of past collaboration. In Asia, relationship can have

In Asia, relationship can have up to four dimensions of meaning.

up to four dimensions of meaning, depending on the specific Asian market:

- To have a *familiarity and comfort level between the parties*

- To be mutually committed to the best interests of the *joint business project*

- To be mutually committed to the *interests of the companies* involved

- To be mutually committed for the *long term*

As this book illuminates, each Asian nation is located on a different place on that relationship spectrum, resulting in relationship having varying degrees of import and impact on negotiating in Asia. See Figure 6 below.

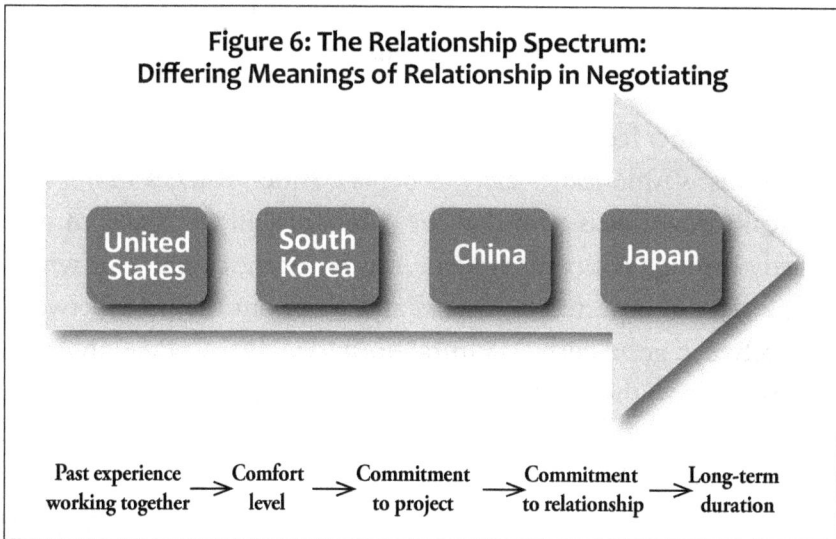

Figure 6: The Relationship Spectrum: Differing Meanings of Relationship in Negotiating

Source: Robert Charles Azar

Given this profound difference in the meaning and importance of relationship in business between America and Asia, it is imperative that U.S. executives be fully aware of and prepared to deal with this difference—its subtleties as well as its substance. A cultural facilitator plays an essential role in that regard as examined in chapter five.

I have witnessed numerous cases where Asian executives ceased negotiations and walked away leaving millions of dollars on the table because they were not able to develop the requisite relationship with foreign companies. As I was able to develop relationships with these executives over time and able to discuss this with them, the reason they would give is that the business is not worth it. They explained that since their interest is in long-term success, knowing that both parties are committed to the relationship as well as the project for the long term is essential. Their concern is without such a dual commitment, how could they discuss and resolve the multiplicity of issues that inevitably arise over time in a business venture in ways that are best for the two companies and their mutual business?

Another factor at play is that Asian markets are nowhere near as litigious as American society. When a business reaches an impasse or breaks down, it is common for companies in the States to seek remedy through the court system. This is not the case in Asia where the parties are expected to discuss and work out the issue between themselves in good faith, a cultural norm deeply imbedded in Asian societies due to the centuries-old emphasis on social harmony.

Even in Asian countries with viable rule of law societies, litigation actions are looked down upon by society. Instead, customary social values of harmony and mutual connection require companies to resolve their differences between them. (For more on mutual connection, see chapter four.) This is why Asian nations have considerably fewer lawyers than America does. Japan, for example, has forty percent of our population, but they have only five percent of the number of attorneys as the U.S.

Given the customary need to work out differences of opinion between business partners in good faith, it is an essential prerequisite that companies forge a relationship sufficient to make that possible. All of these factors contribute to relationship being a dealmaker or deal breaker in Asian negotiating as well as in the degree of compromise necessary in negotiation in Asia.

III. BUSINESS AGREEMENTS: FIXED VS. FLUID

In the U.S., once the terms of a business project are finalized in a signed agreement, the terms are basically set in stone. Because each item of the negotiation was examined and decided upon sequentially and one at a time using linear logic, each item option decided upon represents the best possible option. Accordingly, there is no reason to alter it. It is understood and expected that the major terms will not be renegotiated once they have been agreed upon. Only in extraordinary circumstances would parties to an agreement seek to change them.

Western executives will find that this is not the case in Asia. In China and Korea, for instance, it is quite common for companies to want to change major business terms that have already been agreed to in an agreement after the fact. This is true even long after the business project has commenced. In fact, it is not unusual for executives to want to renegotiate major business

> The answer lies in the fact that business agreements are viewed as being fluid in much of Asia and not fixed as in the U.S.

terms years after the start of the business. Why is this so? The answer lies in the fact that business agreements are viewed as being fluid in much of Asia and not fixed as in the U.S.

In America, agreements are the framework within and the foundation upon which business is conducted. In short, in the States an agreement provides the complete and final understanding of the business project and how each party must perform. The notion that the agreement totally governs the project and is the final understanding of the participating parties is clearly seen in the fact that one of the last sections of most business agreements in the U.S. states that the agreement represents the full and complete understanding of the parties and supersedes any and all previous discussions, agreements, and understandings, written or oral. The final agreement is "the entire deal," nothing more, nothing less.

In many Asian markets including China and Korea, an agreement merely represents a statement of mutual intent to work together. Accordingly, the terms of the agreement are not fixed but are merely preliminary understandings, with an emphasis on preliminary. Why is this so?

> In many Asian markets, an agreement merely represents a statement of mutual intent to work together.

It is critically important to keep in mind that in the Asian view of agreements and business, greater emphasis is given to the fact that the conditions surrounding a business project will inevitably change over time. The longer companies work together over time, the more likely this will become. Given that Asians engage in business on a long-term basis, it is expected that they will need to adjust the terms of any agreement. This facet is another example of how the long-term outlook in Asian business presents challenges for Western executives.

In addition, as Asian executives utilize a holistic logic rather than linear logic and items are perceived as being interrelated, any item may need to be altered due to changes affecting other items. This is another example of how the holistic outlook in Asian negotiating results in dynamics in negotiating and business that Western companies are not used to.

Furthermore, as business takes place based on the relationship between the parties involved and the mutual business is expected to promote the mutual interests of all the parties, changes in a business partner's circumstances are appropriate reasons to seek revision of an agreement's terms. In such cases, the centrality of relationship in negotiating and business in Asia results in challenges for Western executives.

Given all of these factors, in Asia it is *totally natural and understandable* for the parties to seek to change agreement terms in response to future developments. Their requests to do so do not indicate that their previous agreement to the terms was disingenuous or the result of insufficient planning as is often misunderstood by Western executives. From the Asian perspective, it is illogical to be unable to revise agreement terms after the fact to meet the evolving conditions of business. As Wu Min, a Chinese executive, expressed it to me:

"How can anyone know what the future will bring? The only thing we know about the future is it will be different from today. So, does it make sense to say that in the future we must be bound by terms agreed to today, when those terms may no longer apply to our business?"

"Rational decision-making" by management in America and Asia can be radically dissimilar.

As we can see, "rational decision-making" by management in America and Asia can be radically dissimilar.

In looking at the Korean market, we find a similar view of business agreements. Business agreements are viewed as statements of intent to work together whose major terms may need to be renegotiated as the circumstances of the project evolve. However, while agreements are seen as almost entirely fluid in China, they are not fluid to quite the same degree in Korea.

The situation in Japan is different. Agreements there are viewed as their major terms being fixed, as in the States. However, it is not unheard of for companies to ask if your company would be open to revisit those terms as conditions change. The difference in Japan is that it is a polite query. In China and Korea, it is a demand, and it is expected that you will agree. Part of the reason why business agreements are viewed as being less fluid in Japan and Korea than in China is the result of those two countries having adopted the American system of law as they built their modern economies (Japan after World War II and Korea at the conclusion of the Korean War in 1953) and the U.S.'s influence on business practices in those markets.

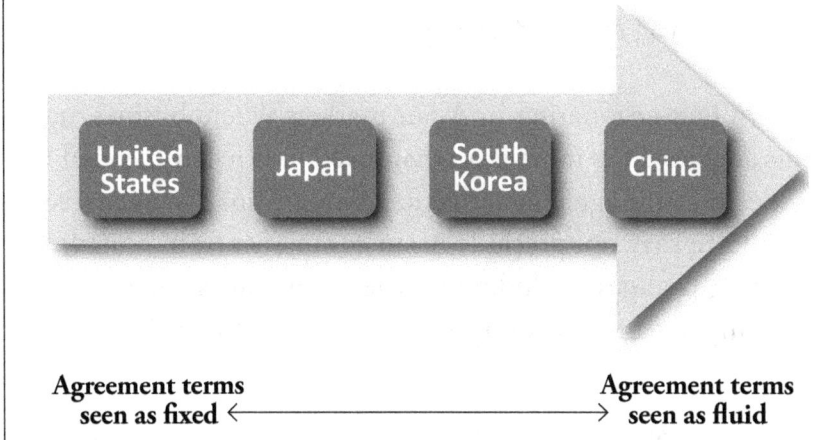

Figure 7: Terms of a Negotiated Agreement: Fixed vs. Flexible

United States — Japan — South Korea — China

Agreement terms seen as fixed ⟷ Agreement terms seen as fluid

Source: Robert Charles Azar

The terms that Asian companies most commonly want to renegotiate include:

- *Pricing* – In addition to the customary reason of remaining competitive, revised pricing requests are often prompted by fluctuations in the exchange rate between the U.S. dollar and the Asian country's currency.

- *Quantities* (procurement or purchase) – Typically these may change influenced by major shifts in industry conditions and product sales.

- *Product performance or design* – Due to extremely competitive market conditions, it is necessary for products in multiple industries in Asian markets to be regularly revised in either performance capability or design in order for them to remain competitive.

In some industries, product design and packaging need to be different for each and every season of the year, each and every year.

When negotiating in Asian markets where business agreements are viewed as more fluid than fixed, it is recommended that you specify in the agreement that its terms are final. While agreeing to that term may not preclude Asian companies from nonetheless requesting changes, including that term in your agreement gives your company a fallback position from which to decline.

IV. FLUID MEETING APPOINTMENTS

When I first began to engage in business in the Korean market, I was surprised to learn that not only are business agreements considered fluid but that appointments are likewise not firm commitments. Time after time I would make appointments to meet with company owners or executives only to experience them not showing up. Not only did they not honor the appointments, they did not even call to say they would not be able to keep the appointment or ask to reschedule it.

Sensing my frustration with this situation, one day Mr. Nam, the native Korean businessman who assisted me in running my company's business in Korea, explained that appointments are not fixed meetings but are simply expressions of an interest to work together. They are just like agreements in this regard. While true more of small- and medium-sized companies than large professional corporations, it is an interesting characteristic of the Korean market that Western executives need to be cognizant of.

How can American executives deal with this fluid and uncertain nature of meeting appointments in Korea? I have found three measures that work well.

First, it is worth the effort to send a fax—not an email— one or two days in advance confirming a meeting. I do not recommend sending an email as it will be hidden in the in-box of the executive and only be seen by him. He may or may not even bother to read it or reply. Sending a fax will result in the executive's staff seeing it. Now it becomes an official company event.

The staff is likely to add the appointment to the executive's calendar. In addition, when they discuss the fax with the executive, the meeting takes on new importance. It graduates from merely being a polite statement from you to the one executive to being an official company activity involving other members of the firm.

Second, have a Korean speaking member of your team call the executive to confirm the meeting the day before. Being able to read the nuances of their own native business culture, that person will be able to more accurately ascertain whether the meeting is simply an expression of interest or a firm appointment. This is another example of the importance of the facilitator interpreter that is discussed in chapter five. In the event you do not have a native speaker on your negotiating team, the duty manager or concierge professional at the hotel where you are staying will be happy to assist you. I have utilized this option numerous times throughout Asia and never had any unwillingness on their part to help. Since you are a guest at their hotel, they see assisting with this as part of their service to keep you a satisfied customer.

Third, set the venue for the meeting at the Korean executive's location. This is especially effective for initial meetings with a company. Doing so precludes the executive from "not showing up"—you are at his/her office. He will certainly meet with you at that time, if he is in. If Mr. Pak, for instance, is out of the office and you show up rightfully saying that you have an appointment with him, the entire staff is embarrassed to the point where they will immediately track down Mr. Pak and have him return to the company to meet with you. It is one way in which U.S. executives can "play the foreigner card"!

I can recall one occasion when I showed up at a Korean company even though my appointment had not been finalized. I really needed to meet with a certain Korean company on behalf of a client, and their executive, Mr. Kim, mentioned he could meet at 10:00 a.m. on either of two dates. While he stated he would contact me beforehand to finalize the date, he never did. Nor did he take or reply to my phone calls or emails to confirm the date. As my time in Korea on that particular trip was coming to an end and meeting with Mr. Kim's company was quite important, I decided just to show up at his office at 10:00 a.m. on the first of the two dates. While he was surprised when I arrived there, he led me into a conference room, and we conducted our meeting as if everything was proceeding just as planned.

It should be noted that while meeting appointments commonly are fluid with small- and medium-sized companies in the Korean market, this is not a factor in China or Japan. This is one more example of how far from uniform the practices of negotiating and business are from one Asian market to another.

V. COMPANY-TO-COMPANY VS. PERSON-TO-PERSON NEGOTIATING

Another fundamental area of difference in global negotiating regards who actually conducts the negotiation. I have found three basic patterns:

Option One: Company-to-Company. Negotiations take place on a strictly company-to-company basis. That is, the negotiation between the two parties is organization to organization and is conducted by the negotiating team of each firm. Changes in the composition of the individual members of the negotiating teams or the company's executives have little or no effect on the length or outcome of the negotiations. While new individuals may end up negatively impacting a negotiation for any number of reasons, the act of changing individuals itself has little effect—the negotiations are taking place between organizations, not between any certain individuals.

Option Two: Individual-to-Individual. Negotiating takes place primarily on an individual-to-individual basis. While the companies involved may send teams to the negotiation to represent them, in actuality the negotiating takes place between one key individual on each team. Rather than between the two teams, the negotiation is conducted primarily by those key individuals. In the end, their interactions constitute the bulk of negotiation. Progress in the negotiation depends on progress between the primary negotiators.

In the event one of those key individuals is replaced, the negotiation can be significantly impacted. The new person must be able to replace the previous key individual in his/her role as primary negotiator and be able to make progress with their primary negotiator counterpart. As having a comfort level with the other party is a minimum threshold of relationship throughout Asia, the negotiations can stall or fall apart if a comfort level is not formed between the new key individual and the counterpart key negotiator. The inability of the two individuals to work together can effectively jeopardize the negotiation.

Option Three: Team Spokesperson. In the team spokesman approach, a hybrid of options one and two, negotiating takes place both on a company-to-company level as well as between key individuals. While key individuals in this scenario may lead the discussions as in option two, they do so more as a team spokesperson and not as primary negotiator, and fellow team members are substantively involved throughout the course of the negotiations. In this way, the negotiation has the stability of option one with the consequence that replacing individual members of the negotiating team likely will not negatively impact the negotiations.

In America, parties engaged in negotiating generally relate to each other in the manner of option one or three—that is, on a company-to-company basis or hybrid pattern. Accordingly, when the individuals comprising the negotiating team change, that has little or no effect on the length or outcome of the discussions.

In the Japanese and Korean markets, all facets of business including negotiations are conducted on a group basis; that is option one. Negotiating team members can be interchanged throughout the course of a negotiation without consequence to its outcome in Japan and Korea. It is important to note, however, that while this applies in Korea to medium- and large-sized companies, small businesses can utilize either the company-to-company style or be dominated by one person. This is especially likely if the company is run by its owner.

In China, it is very different. The role of the individual primary negotiator is much greater in the overall negotiation as in option two. Despite China's Confucianism-based harmony that is prevalent throughout Asian societies, resistance to teamwork (group harmony) in a business context is quite common. Consequently, replacing key members of the negotiating team can greatly influence a negotiation.

In the case the company you are negotiating with utilizes option two or three, it is critically important to ascertain who has the decision-making authority on their negotiating team. The individual leading the discussion is not necessarily the decision maker. Likewise, the apparent decision maker may not be the actual decision maker. Let's look at a rather dramatic historical example of this.

When America and Vietnam engaged in the Paris peace talks to negotiate the end of the Vietnam war, the negotiating team representing Vietnam was led by one person who acted as if he was the decision maker in attendance at the meeting. However, he was not. Instead with this point man on the Vietnamese negotiating team busy engaging the U.S. negotiators and doing all the talking, the actual decision maker sitting off to the side was free to quietly give all of his attention to consider the substance of what was being discussed, strategize about it, and formulate a response. The decision maker would signal the apparent Vietnamese negotiating team leader with his cigarette lighter that he always had on the table in front of him. Holding the lighter vertically signaled a "yes" reply to the lead negotiator while placing the lighter horizontally meant "no." It took the U.S. negotiating team several months to realize who was actually the decision-maker at the negotiation.

American executives can always directly ask the other company's negotiators who the decision maker present at the negotiating meeting is. This will clarify which of the three options they are following. In addition, it pays to be observant not only of the manner with which the other negotiating team interacts with your company but also of any intra-team communication that takes place among them during the negotiation discussions, especially their non-verbal communication.

While it is important to know this as early in the negotiations as possible, I have found that asking at the very outset is often perceived as being too direct by Asian executives. Inquiring instead after the negotiations are under way goes over smoothly and is productive. For example, if your negotiations are scheduled from 9:00 a.m. to 1:00 p.m. and divided into two sessions with a short break between them, raise this question as you conclude the first session. Doing so affords you the opportunity to follow up in a one-on-one conversation during the break with their decision-maker.

VI. DECISION-MAKING IN NEGOTIATING

In America, decision-making is conducted in a top down fashion. The senior most person calls the shots and what is decided is communicated to those affected by it for implementation. It is not uncommon for those impacted by those decisions to hear about them for the first time after the decision has already been made, and in some cases, they first hear about a decision at the time of implementation.

Different options may be discussed; different approaches may be recommended by the heads of the various departments involved; other pros and cons may be interjected by other participants in the discussions; however, in the end, it is the senior most executive involved in the decision-making process who makes the decision for the company. Once the decision is made, it is passed down to all relevant parties in the company for execution. In this way, decision-making takes place at the top of the organization and flows down to the rank and file in a top down fashion in most American companies.

There are two major types of decision-making in Asian nations. First, countries such as China and Thailand also utilize a top down method of decision-making just as we do in the States. Second, in Japan, Korea, Singapore, Indonesia, and Vietnam, a quite different type of decision-making is used, namely a group-oriented method.

Within Asia, group decision-making is most pronounced in the Japanese market. It is a very involved, meticulous, and time-intense method where, in addition to being a group effort, decision-making is also a bottom up process. All parties involved with the decision and its ramifications are included in the discussions from the very beginning and in every step throughout the entire decision-making process. Here is how it typically works in Japan.

A proposal will be circulated to all of those departments or parties who will be affected as well as those who should be aware of the matter to be decided, such as senior executives. Each party will take as much time as they need to thoroughly review the proposal, closely looking at three fundamental considerations:

- **Proposal's effectiveness:** Is the proposal the best way to achieve its stated objective and intended purpose from the perspective of each individual stakeholder? If not, ways to maximize the proposal's effectiveness and efficiencies are formulated and added by each party concerned.

- **Proposal's requirements:** What will each department need to do to comply with the proposal? Each department will identify, define, and analyze the specifics of this as it considers the proposal.

- **Proposal's impact:** How will the proposal impact each individual party? What will be the impact on productivity rates, quality control, cost, workload, employee morale, sales, and the company's competitive standing in the market? Each department will offer ways to avoid, or at least minimize, negative impact(s) the proposal may have and also will offer ways to maximize its benefits. After that, each individual party will examine how the proposal will impact their interactions with other departments within their company as well as stakeholders outside of the firm such as suppliers, vendors, and customers.

After concluding this initial review of the proposal, each participating group will add the results of their review to the proposal. The revised proposal document will then be circulated again to all groups involved. Each group goes through subsequent reviews of the document as the additions of all the other groups are added, each time again checking the proposal's requirements, effectiveness, and impact. Once all parties have reviewed and revised the proposal to best take into consideration their situation, the content of the proposal becomes finalized. The head of each department involved in this process stamps the seal of his department on it (literally), signifying that the department has officially approved the proposal's content. The proposal must be approved in that way by each and every department involved for the decision to be adopted.

Decisions are thus made by consensus. This requires all departments to work together to ensure the needs and interests of each and every department involved are addressed. Just as we saw in chapter one that negotiating *between companies* involves taking into account the business interests of both companies, internal decision-making likewise requires allowing for the business interests of the other departments *within a company*. Accordingly, taking into account the interests of other parties applies both to *intracompany* as well as *intercompany* negotiating and business. This decision-making dynamic is based upon harmony and the strong group orientation in the business culture and management practices of Asian countries. It permeates the approach to negotiating in Japan and other Asian markets.

> Taking into account the interests of other parties applies both to intracompany as well as intercompany negotiating and business.

This method of involving all parties affected by a proposal in the group decision-making process from the very start and throughout every step of the decision-making process is used to the greatest degree in Asia in the Japanese market. There it is called *ringi* (稟議). Figure 8 below illustrates the Japanese version of the group decision-making process.

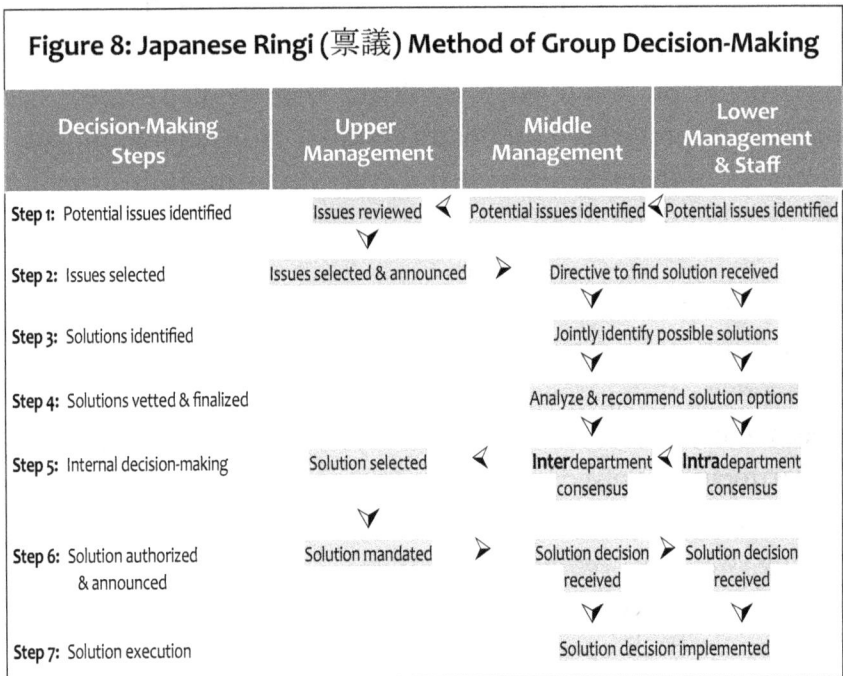

Figure 8: Japanese Ringi (稟議) Method of Group Decision-Making			
Decision-Making Steps	**Upper Management**	**Middle Management**	**Lower Management & Staff**
Step 1: Potential issues identified	Issues reviewed ◄	Potential issues identified ◄	Potential issues identified
Step 2: Issues selected	Issues selected & announced ➤	Directive to find solution received	
Step 3: Solutions identified		Jointly identify possible solutions	
Step 4: Solutions vetted & finalized		Analyze & recommend solution options	
Step 5: Internal decision-making	Solution selected ◄	**Inter**department consensus ◄	**Intra**department consensus
Step 6: Solution authorized & announced	Solution mandated ➤	Solution decision received ➤	Solution decision received
Step 7: Solution execution		Solution decision implemented	

Source: Robert Charles Azar

As one can easily imagine, this process is very tedious and requires considerable time. However, the advantages of this method of group decision-making outweigh the disadvantages. Let's look at some of the major advantages.

Because each group or department of the company affected by a proposal is continuously involved in the decision-making process from beginning to end, they are all fully knowledgeable about the proposal contents when implementation time comes. They all are keenly aware of what the proposal will require of them, how it will impact them, and what practical steps they will need to take to prepare for and execute it. As a result, they are fully informed and ready to implement the proposal as soon as the decision is finalized.

Since all the relevant parties include their recommendations in the decision and give it their approval, they have a sense of ownership and responsibility regarding the outcome of the decision. They have skin in the game, so to speak. Consequently, once it is time to implement the decision, each participating party has a vested interest in making sure the decision is implemented as successfully as possible. As a result, another benefit of Asian group decision-making is that rarely is there any implementation resistance to new decisions or the changes they necessitate.

In contrast, in a top down decision-making process such as in the States, the affected parties often start to examine what is required of them, how it will impact them, and what changes will be required *after* the decision has been made and announced. This often causes a delay between the time a decision is announced and when it can be implemented. In addition, as the affected parties were not involved in the decision, there are occasions when they resist implementing the decision because it may have detrimental effects on them. Even worse, new initiatives and their requisite changes may be sabotaged or outright ignored by managers who deem them not in the best interest of their department or their own personal career.

In summary, while group decision-making in Asian companies may take more time than decision-making in American companies, the implementation of the decision takes place in a manner that is quicker, smoother, and more comprehensive by having all parties affected by a decision fully engaged in the decision-making process. In contrast, the U.S. top down decision-making method allows for decisions to be made much faster. However, the decision's implementation can be slower and less effective for several reasons:

- The parties affected by a decision often only hear about a decision after it has been made, sometimes only at implementation time. As a result, they feel no ownership toward the decision and may not feel as responsible for or committed to implementing it.

- When parties affected by a decision only hear about it after the fact, they are unfamiliar with the proposal's expectations. They need time to understand the requirements and costs, formulate steps to execute them, and then actually implement the decision.

- The parties may not have everything needed to implement the proposal readily available and may need time to source and prepare them for implementation.

- In cases where the proposal is likely to cause changes or have a negative impact on a department's performance, the department head can resist—or outright derail—implementation to avoid their department taking a performance hit. Such turf wars can be costly to a company in many ways and negatively impact the company's business both short and long term.

As the Asian group method of decision-making requires a greater amount of time, understandably, negotiations in those countries take longer as a result. U.S. negotiators need to keep this fundamental difference in mind in their approach to and planning for negotiations in those markets. In addition, it is another reason why expecting to having your sales agreement signed during your initial meeting with an Asian partner is not realistic in most countries in that region.

As the Asian group method of decision-making requires a greater amount of time, negotiations take longer as a result.

VII. TIME IN NEGOTIATION

A. PACE AND LENGTH OF NEGOTIATING

From the very first negotiating session with Asian executives, it becomes clear that they engage in negotiating at a much slower pace than Americans do. As has been presented, this stems from the fact that Americans and Asians view both the purpose and process of negotiating in fundamentally different ways.

To reiterate, typically Americans have a list of objectives that are central to the business opportunity that we want to discuss and come to agreement on—that is the primary focus of the negotiation. We expect the negotiations to proceed in a straightforward and time-efficient manner. If they do not, we take that to be an indication that something is off target—that the other party is not really interested, agreement may not be possible, or the other company possibly has ulterior motives.

For Asians, we have already identified that the negotiation process takes place on two distinct levels: project and relationship. While Americans approach negotiating with the one primary objective of coming to agreement on the major points of the business deal, Asians pursue three major objectives through the negotiating process. And they pursue them simultaneously. As a result, the Asian negotiating process is far more involved and requires significantly more time than the American approach.

As a reminder from chapter one, here are the three major business objectives Asian companies simultaneously pursue through the negotiating process:

- Becoming well informed about the project and products

- Building a constructive, long-term working relationship with the other party

- Coming to agreement on the particulars of the business deal not only with the company they are negotiating with but also simultaneously arriving at a consensus on these points within their own company

As an example, let's look at each of these three facets in Japanese negotiating in detail where these traits are the most pronounced.

Japanese conduct negotiations in a meticulous fashion. This is part of their exact, cautious, and detail-oriented approach known in Japanese as *komakai* (細かい). This is most commonly seen in the level of detail Japanese request on the business project during the course of negotiating—the first of the three negotiating objectives noted above.

The detail they typically ask for is far more than Americans require or even consider reasonable. From an American perspective, it often seems like information overkill. I have witnessed numerous cases where American executives wondered if their Japanese counterparts were simply seeking all this detailed information for the purpose of "knocking off" the American product. However, as a general rule, this is not what is taking place.

Japanese require this enormous amount of detail in negotiating because they want to be as thorough as possible in their work. They prefer to know as much as possible up front during the negotiating process in order to avoid surprises down the road. Finding out after the business commences that they were not sufficiently informed or that they outright made a mistake causes loss of face, the worst possible stigma in Japanese social and business culture. For them, it is better to err on the side of being overly cautious by being overly informed than risk having themselves and their company experience loss of face because of a failure to obtain all the necessary information. As a traditional Japanese proverb puts it:

Better a moment's embarrassment in asking than a lifetime of shame for not having asked.

Chinese likewise are usually well prepared for all

negotiations. Accordingly, they also request great amounts of information during negotiating sessions so as to be well informed and best able to make prudent decisions. In contrast to this cautious "look before you leap" attitude found in China and Japan, Korean negotiators are more willing to leap first and worry about the details later. This is part of the *ppalli-ppalli* (hurry, hurry) culture discussed in chapter one.

As noted earlier, loss of face and dishonoring one's company in Asia is equivalent to having your credibility, integrity, and standing in society called into question or destroyed in American culture. Asian business men and women will go to great lengths to avoid this. Looking back to pre-modern Japan, for example, the samurai values of *Bushido* would call on a samurai who lost his honor to commit *seppuku* (切腹ceremonial disembowelment). In modern Japan, an executive's loss of face or dishonor requires the executive to take responsibility by resigning his position and leaving the company. That is why executive resignations are commonly seen in Japan in the aftermath of corporate scandals or other actions that embarrass a company.

In addition, being well-informed generally strengthens a party's bargaining position in negotiations. This notion is common throughout the world—"Knowledge is power" as Francis Bacon aptly noted—and is an integral part of negotiating in Asia.

It is interesting to point out some differences in the purpose for which Chinese and Japanese request information in negotiations. While Chinese negotiators also arrive well-prepared, during the actual negotiation they prefer information needed to understand the matter immediately at hand. Japanese negotiators seek information not only on matters immediately at hand but also on the project at large, generally requiring significantly more information than in other Asian countries.

Likewise, it is common for both Chinese and Japanese negotiators to question everything. However, doing so in China is a negotiating tactic to wear down foreigners who are usually tired from their long journey there and the resulting jet lag and who feel the pressure of being in China for a very limited amount of time. The Chinese tactic of utilizing constant questioning as a means to wear down a visiting negotiating team is different from the Japanese practice of asking seemingly endless questions. There, it is a means to understand as much about the entire business as possible to avoid being unprepared or surprised in the future. Also, being well informed about the entire project is a necessary facet of the holistic view Asians take in negotiating, as discussed in chapter one.

It is noteworthy that in Japan, the amount of information exchanged has tremendous value not only for the purpose of being well-informed about the project but also for the purposes of relationship building— the second of the three negotiating objectives noted above. The breadth and depth of information exchanged is an important indicator of how serious parties are about working together and trusting each other. The stronger the relationship, the greater the amount of information that is exchanged. All of these traits are essential elements in building a trust relationship in the Japanese market.

> The amount of information exchanged has tremendous value for the purposes of relationship building.

American companies typically do not have pre-existing relationships with Asian companies so the important process of relationship building must take place during the negotiations. This adds a whole other unfamiliar dimension to the negotiating process for the foreign company; one that requires considerable time, effort, and attention in addition to the time, effort, and attention being spent on negotiating the specific points of the business—the third of the three negotiating objectives noted above.

Recognizing that the now familiar internal bottom-up decision-making process must also occur in the negotiating process, the question is when does it occur? It takes place between meetings with potential business partners. This factor is another reason why Asian companies proceed in negotiating at a speed considerably slower than American companies.

> American executives have found the longer and more involved negotiating process with Asian companies to be daunting.

I have encountered American executives who have found the longer and more involved negotiating process with Asian companies to be daunting. Is it worth it to be patient and go through this much longer negotiating process?

The most obvious point is that being unwilling to accommodate the need for greater negotiating time will prevent your company from completing a business agreement for Asian markets. Simply put, not allowing for the necessary time for negotiating in Asia would be to fail in Asian markets even before you had the opportunity to start your business there.

When we step back and strategically analyze this longer and more involved negotiating process of Asian companies, it is clear that the process offers American companies distinct advantages that are well worth the extra time. I have found the following three fundamental advantages for American companies to be especially noteworthy:

- In the case of Japan and other Asian markets, the need to be so meticulous, detail oriented, and well informed during the negotiation process puts your Asian partners in a very strong position to sell and service your products in their markets from day one of project launch. I have been involved in countless projects in which Japanese actually ended up understanding the business or product even better than the Western manufacturer.

- Asian companies are generally committed to the project for the long term and, as a result, typically have greater staying power than partners in other countries. Since business is conducted based on the long-term relationship between the two parties, the bottom line benefit to you of this cultural trait is that Asian partners typically will continue to promote your products even if or when sales turn out to be slower than anticipated. This feature is most prominent in Japan.

- As a result of the group consensus decision-making process, all parts of the Japanese company that will be involved in your business in Japan are already quite familiar with your product and business and what will be required of them; they are already on board, geared up at the start line, and ready to move forward on a long-term trajectory from the date your business agreement is signed. This provides American executives with three invaluable tactical advantages.

o Your partner will require a shorter ramp up time to prepare for commencement of your business in Japan.

o Your company's launch in the Japanese market will be more comprehensive, informed, effective, and professional given your partner's in-depth knowledge of your products and business gained *before* your business is launched.

o When your product faces challenges in the Japanese market, your partner is in a position to formulate effective hands-on solutions quickly in the field. While your staff certainly will know the products very well, they will not understand the particulars of the Asian markets and the actual challenges your products face in it over time. Asian partners will not only be well informed about your product but also will be intimately familiar with the market challenges. As a result, they are able to contribute real-time solutions in a quick and effective manner to a greater degree than you would find in other international markets.

Briefly returning to the first of these three advantages, I noted that as a result of needing to be so meticulous, detail oriented, and well informed about a product, Japanese can actually end up knowing them even better than the American entity does. Management expert Peter Drucker experienced this himself through his work with Mr. Ueda Atsuo, who translated and edited the Japanese language editions of Drucker's books over the years. As Dr. Drucker noted:

> *"He [Ueda Atsuo] has actually translated many of my books several times as they went into new Japanese editions. He is thus thoroughly familiar with my work—in fact, he knows it better than I do."* — **Peter F. Drucker, *The Essential Drucker* (New York: Harper Collins, 2001), page vii.**

In summary, I have always found regarding Asian negotiating that while the negotiation process may be long, it increases the quality and value of the resulting business relationship and business project between American firms and their Asian partners.

B.   TIME AS A NEGOTIATING TOOL

Some Asian companies use time as a tool to win advantages in the negotiating process, so American companies must be aware of this tactic.

In most cases, the initial negotiation meetings take place in Asia. Typically, the U.S. executive arrives and is there for a few busy days of meetings. No matter how seasoned the executive might be, he or she invariably is fatigued due to the long journey. On top of that, given the fourteen- to seventeen-hour time difference between mainland U.S.A. and Asia, the body clocks of American executives are off during their initial days in Asia.

American executives typically have approximately forty-eight to seventy-two hours in an Asian market to negotiate, a very short window of opportunity. Not only do foreign executives operate on a short time horizon because of the limited time they are in Asia, they are used to negotiations moving forward in a quick and straightforward manner. In the foreign executive's mind, there is an expectation of meaningful progress within a short period of time. On top of that, he or she would like to return to the States and report positive news about the negotiations. I have often experienced U.S. executives showing me their company's sales agreement before meeting with Asian companies and stating that their goal is to have it signed before they leave in a day or two. As we have seen, this is simply not realistic given the dynamics of Asian negotiating and business.

As a result of these factors, the U.S. executive is weighed down with several challenges even before walking into the meeting room to conduct the negotiation. Some of these challenges are:

- **Logistical:** Fatigue from the long journey to Asia (twenty to twenty-two hours door-to-door from the east coast of America to your hotel in downtown Tokyo for example); jet lag from the fourteen- to seventeen-hour time difference between the continental U.S. and Asian markets; and the need to conduct as much business as possible during the short visit put the American executive at an immediate disadvantage.

- **Cultural:** There are numerous culture-based differences in negotiating and business practices such as the much slower pace and more involved process of Asian negotiating. In most cases, American executives are not aware of or accustomed to dealing with these differences and the multiplicity of challenges they present.

- **Expectancy:** There is pressure to report positive news about the negotiations when they return to the U.S. or even to have a signed agreement completed during that visit.

Asian negotiators are well aware of the time restrictions and these other challenges that their American counterparts bring to the negotiating table. While Asians approach negotiating at a much slower pace than Americans do to begin with, some may elect to deliberately slow down the negotiating process even further as a negotiating tactic to frustrate and wear down the other party.

> Asian executives may try to win concessions by dragging out the discussions.

For example, given the desire of the U.S. executive to make progress during the very short window of time for negotiating, Asian executives may try to win concessions by dragging out the discussions. They are betting that as the American executive's stay nears its end, the urge to achieve progress in the limited amount of time the executive has in Asia will prompt compromises and concessions to the advantage of the Asian company.

You can avoid this negotiating tactic by stating at the outset of your initial discussion that you are not in a hurry to conclude an agreement or to report progress to your company headquarters. Instead, take the position that your company is simply looking into the possibility of doing business in that Asian market at this time. Accordingly, the purpose of your visit is purely exploratory and that you want both companies to get to know each other during your visit. Explain that your company is taking a long-term approach to negotiating and to conducting business in Asia. Starting the negotiation with these points makes it known to the Asian company that they cannot use time as a tool against you. In addition, doing so presents your company in a favorable manner by indicating your interest in relationship and long-term approach.

While it is not realistic to expect to have a business agreement signed during your initial visit to most Asian countries, it still is prudent to bring your company's agreement with you to the negotiation. If the Asian company is strongly interested in your company's business opportunity and you are favorably inclined to work with them, you may want to present your business agreement to them at the conclusion of your last meeting for the purpose of allowing them to have it translated into their language so it can be discussed at a future meeting. Present only the boilerplate version of the agreement for this purpose. Do not include the specifics you will be negotiating.

Depending on the length of the agreement, the level of technical content included in it, and the prevalence of specialized terminology it may contain, a translation can take anywhere from a few days to one to two weeks. Having the boilerplate version of your document translated into the Asian language of any country you are negotiating in allows Asian executives the opportunity to become more familiar with the general terms you have in mind before your next negotiating meeting. This often aids in shortening the amount of subsequent time needed to complete the negotiating process.

C. DIFFERENT NOTIONS OF TIME

In assisting American clients engaged in business in Asian markets over the years, I became aware on numerous occasions of noteworthy differences regarding notions of time frames. Here is a prime example.

A business agreement had been negotiated and signed between an American company and its Asian partner, the working relationship continued to develop, regulatory approvals to import and sell products were obtained, and the companies launched the project and began marketing and selling as planned.

Everything seemed to be operating smoothly until after about five or six weeks, the U.S. company inquired about the progress of sales and meeting the target numbers mutually agreed upon. The American executives were concerned that the Asian company was not taking the sales targets seriously, but the Asian executives were puzzled at the impatience of their American partner. To the Asian partner, everything appeared to be on target. What happened here?

Looking into this, it became apparent to me that the two companies were operating with two entirely different understandings of "agreed" time frames. For U.S. clients, short-term was a few months or a few quarters at most. For the Asian firm, short-term was considered much longer—anywhere between eighteen to twenty-four months. What a huge disparity! Given how different the two time frames are, it is easy to see how misunderstandings can occur in the relationship and with evaluating progress in sales performance, marketing, advertising, and so many other areas of business.

To avoid these problems when negotiating, it is important to understand the meaning of short term, midterm, and long term in the markets of both companies.

The frameworks for time common in America are:

- **Short term:** Measured in weeks, months, or quarters. Typically, up to six or nine months

- **Midterm:** Nine to eighteen months

- **Long term:** Eighteen months or longer

In Asia, while the time frames vary in length from industry to industry, they are all considerably longer than in the States. In Japan, for example, the following time frames are an average of these time periods:

- **Short term:** One-and-a-half to two years

- **Midterm:** Three to four years

- **Long term:** Five years and beyond

As we can see, the time frames Asian and American

business professionals bring to the negotiating table are markedly different. The same terms are used, but their cultural meanings are significantly different. This is true even when Asians negotiate in English; while they may use the same English term "short term," their cultural understanding and their expectations are quite different.

> The time frames Asian and American business professionals bring to the negotiating table are markedly different.

This is a case of accurate literal translation but inaccurate cultural interpretation. There are occasions when Asians will negotiate in English so that both they and American negotiators are speaking the same language. Executives of both countries feel a sense of relief with this, believing that, as a result, misunderstandings are less likely since nothing can "get lost in translation." While it is true that there is less risk of the literal meaning being misunderstood when both sides are speaking in English, the actual cultural meaning and expectation still often get lost in translation. The result is without intending to, both sides are setting themselves up for misunderstandings, friction in their business relationship, and diminished business results. This is true not only with regard to understanding time frame terms but also with numerous facets of business.

While common ideas and terms in international business that come up in business negotiations and subsequent management of the joint business venture may be the same, the cultural connotations quite often are very different. Because these cultural connotations are subconscious and taken for granted, negotiators and managers on both sides are usually unaware that differences exist between them.

> There is a monumental difference between having accurate language translation and achieving correct cultural interpretation.

The critical lesson for international business executives is that there is a monumental difference between having accurate language translation and achieving correct cultural interpretation both during the negotiating process and during the course of the joint business project.

This aspect of negotiating and communication—that is, having both accurate language translation and correct cultural interpretation—is critical to the success of a foreign company's business in Asia, yet it is usually overlooked by management on both sides of the Pacific. I have experienced time and again how this gap in understanding can emerge at any point—even after several years—in the business project.

The importance of obtaining correct cultural interpretation between American and Asian negotiators along with accurate language interpretation highlights the need to have a facilitator interpreter and is covered in depth in chapters four and five.

To avoid this cultural miscommunication during negotiations, it is always preferable to quantify terms and concepts whenever possible. In the example above, for instance, the use of numerical time periods (such as one year) instead of terms for time frames (such as short term, midterm, or long term) would have resulted in clearer expectations for the companies. Other commonly used and misunderstood terms for time frames include "in phase one," "in the initial stage," "for a while," and "in the interim." Business interests are always best served by defining and quantifying all terms and concepts whenever possible—even when discussed in English by both parties.

Not quantifying can result in several unwelcome consequences. First, misunderstandings occur regarding completion dates and achievement of project milestones. Second, misunderstandings occur due to operating with different time assumptions, which causes friction in the relationship between the two companies. Not working with the same timetable can lead a company to think the other party is not carrying out its end of the bargain or, conversely, to feel the business partner is harassing them when they feel they are in compliance with the agreement. Commitment to and involvement in the business project can suffer as a result, eroding sales performance. This is another clear example of how possessing or not possessing appropriate cultural understanding directly impacts the bottom line performance of international business operations.

D. RESPECT FOR TIME

In Asia, the value of time is greatly respected as is being punctual. This is true both in business and in society in general. As a result, being late is unacceptable. In America, we are a bit more relaxed about punctuality. Being "socially late" is quite common, and if we are a few minutes late to a business meeting, it is not usually a serious matter. Unpunctuality in the business world in most of Asia, especially Japan, is out of the question. You are expected to be on time for all appointments and engagements.

Being late indicates that not only do you not respect the value of time but also that you do not respect the other party.

In the business context, being late translates culturally as being unreliable—and therefore undesirable—as a potential business partner. Punctuality is that important. This is especially true during the courtship phase when American and Asian companies are getting to know each other to decide whether or not to work together. Given this great respect for time and the importance of being on time, the common practice is to arrive for appointments fifteen to thirty minutes early and wait nearby the meeting venue until the appointed time.

But there is more. Respecting time means being on time—but being on time only! Arriving early at the meeting location is likewise not done. It is common in Asia that when a company has an appointment with another company and assures on-time arrival by arriving early, the representatives wait in the building's lobby or a nearby coffee shop until the meeting time approaches. They then proceed to the company's reception area exactly at the appointed time. To arrive at the reception area before the appointed meeting time is considered disrespectful of the other party and their time since the people you are meeting with certainly are busy taking care of other matters. To meet you early would interfere with their responsibilities and planned agenda for the day. As a result, Asians arrive at the reception area just on time.

> The "just in time" concept Japanese perfected in manufacturing and inventory practices applies to meeting protocol as well.

This trait is especially true in Japan, part of their predilection for being exact and detail-oriented (*komakai* 細かい) as discussed earlier. You may have heard of the "just in time" concept Japanese perfected in manufacturing and inventory practices—it applies to meeting protocol as well.

Respect for time in general and for the other party's time in particular is so important in Japan that people actually apologize for keeping you waiting even though they are on time and, therefore, have not kept you waiting! The ubiquitous Japanese expression is *o-matase-itashimashita* (お待たせいたしました) and means "Sorry to have kept you waiting." Japanese will say this upon arriving for any engagement, including when entering a meeting room exactly at the appointed meeting time. My favorite example of the use of this phrase is when a train closes its doors and starts to pull out of a station, the conductor invariably says over the intercom "Sorry to have kept you waiting"—despite the fact that the train is precisely on schedule. Another example of how Asians respect time.

E.   COMMITMENT TO THE LONG TERM

The last aspect of time that comes to play in the negotiating process and in business in general in Asia is the importance of the long term. Unlike Western companies, Asians approach business with a long-term view. They strategize and plan for the long term. They allocate resources, train employees, invest in research and development, and engage in customer service all with the long term in mind. In a nutshell, Asian companies engage in business for the long term so all aspects of business have a long-term orientation and trajectory. Given this cultural norm and the need to commit so many resources, it is very important to them that they can see that your commitment is likewise long term for both the joint business as well as the mutual relationship.

If a foreign company is going to cease business in Asia

because sales were below expectations for a few quarters—here today, gone tomorrow—Asian executives believe why bother even to start the business? It will turn out to be a waste of time, effort, and investment for both companies. Furthermore, this is problematic and often causes the Asian company "to lose face" on two levels:

- **In their industry among their peer companies:** Prestige and perceived standing among their competitors often suffer as a result of come and go associations.

- **In public society in general:** The exit of the foreign company leaves the Asian company in a difficult situation. Officially they are no longer engaged in that business and have shut down those operations. However, the Asian company often remains socially obligated to continue servicing any and all customers who have purchased those products even after operations cease. Unlike in America, this is socially expected of companies in Asia. With the Western company no longer active there, it becomes highly problematic and costly to handle any customer inquiries, complaints, maintenance, warranty issues, after-purchase product service needs, and repairs with no back up from the foreign manufacturer and no sales income from that project.

These concerns make it clear why Asian negotiators pay attention to your company's level of commitment to their market for the long term. This can have a direct and significant impact on negotiations regarding how Asian companies select both the project partner and the sales targets for your business.

When negotiating, American executives tend to push for sales targets that are as high as possible. Asians often resist and want sales targets that are lower. The reason for this is not that their commitment to the project is weak or that they see lower sales potential than their foreign counterparts see, or even that they simply tend to be more conservative than American executives as it is commonly explained in the West. Rather, the reason is that the lower the target numbers, the more likely it is that they will be achieved and keep American executives satisfied. And, more importantly, that successfully meeting sales goals will keep the American company wanting to continue its business in the Asian market longer.

Considering this, it is highly recommended that U.S. companies pursuing business in Asia proactively bring up the topic of their commitment to the market. As already mentioned, it is advantageous to initiate and openly discuss this commitment early on in the negotiations. This is especially true if your company is competing with other foreign or even domestic Asian companies to work with your target company.

> It is highly recommended that U.S. companies pursuing business in Asia proactively bring up the topic of their commitment to the market.

Given the importance of taking this stance, how can American companies effectively express to Asian companies that their commitment to the market and to the mutual business relationship is both strong and long term? Here are five specific methods that have been proven successful for my clients:

- **Geographic importance of the Asian market:** Discuss not only the additional sales you expect from your business in the Asian market but also cover the *geographic significance* of the market to your company. For example, explain how your firm sees the market of the company you are negotiating with as the gateway to or model for other Asian countries, so succeeding there will enable your company to expand more easily into those other neighboring markets. This indicates to the Asian company that your succeeding in their market is integral to your firm's broader strategy for Asia.

- **Strategic importance of the Asian market:** Explain the *strategic significance* of the market to your business. For example, discuss how it is a major market in the world for your product or service and, consequently, your succeeding there is an integral part of your company's strategy to be the global leader in its product category.

- **Your company's team for that Asian market:** Point out how you are creating a whole team within your company to manage your business with your Asian partner in their market. Explain this team will not be comprised just of members from your international sales department. That is not compelling enough. Instead, demonstrate that your team will include senior executives and managers from the various departments of your company who will be actively involved in your company's business there.

This would include, for example, sales, marketing, regulatory affairs, customer service, human resources, procurement, quality control, research and development, and finance. All of these individuals will be working to meet the needs of your partner's market—not just the director of international sales and his/her department. This approach demonstrates that your effort in the Asian market will be company-wide and not just the work of part of your international sales department. From the perspective of Asian companies, the greater the level of the personnel and other corporate resources your team includes in their country, the more serious and long term your commitment is to their market.

Taking this stance requires that company members from those various departments attend meetings with Asian executives. They do not have to attend all the negotiating meetings, but when the Asian company visits your office for meetings, the senior-most executives from those various departments should attend. Their presence sends a powerful and clear message that the Asian market is a priority for your company. While this may take a few hours of their time, it will be well worth it in terms of the long-term benefit your company will earn through a strong relationship with its Asian partner.

- **On-going business support:** Discuss details of how after the project commences, your company will continue to provide product training and support to your Asian partner on an on-going basis for the long term. That support will include teams of appropriate professionals from your company visiting several times a year (or other frequency appropriate to your company's resources and the specific needs of the business project) to working side-by-side with your Asian partner and the customers they develop.

- **On-going executive level communication:** Explain how you and other senior executives will maintain direct, personal communication with the senior executives of the Asian company on a regular basis going forward. That will include face-to-face meetings in their market as well as in the United States, meetings via Skype and other similar technologies, as well as telephone conversations. Remember that for Asian executives your business with them is relationship driven. You should be proactive in demonstrating that your relationship with them is both long-term and a high priority. This will go a long way to giving them the comfort level to want to work with your company and be fully committed to your business in their country.

All of these actions send the clear message that you and your company take your relationship with the Asian company seriously, that you are committed to them and their market, and that your goal is to be in that market with them for the long term. These messages will help give Asian executives the requisite comfort level to move forward in negotiating with your company.

INSIGHTS

This chapter examined how Asian negotiating dynamics differ so fundamentally from those that drive negotiations in the States, including the following twelve items:

- The central role of relationship in negotiating

- The varying definitions and implications of relationship

- The differing importance of relationship in negotiating

- The ways business relationships are initiated

- The actions required for maintaining relationships

- The different meaning and use of compromise, concession, and bargaining

- The way in which business agreements are viewed as fluid and open to further negotiations after the fact

- The manner in which meeting appointments are often not firm commitments

- The differences between company-to-company negotiating and person-to-person negotiating

- The specifics of the different decision-making methods

- The role and importance of time in Asian negotiating

- The tactics American executives can utilize to demonstrate long-term commitment to your Asian partner and your business in their market

Table 1: Divergent Negotiating Dynamics

Trait	China	Japan	Korea	America
Time orientation in business and negotiating	Long term	Long term	Short term	Short term
Focus in business and negotiating	Self-interest	Mutual interest	Self-interest	Self-interest
Business driver	Transaction then relationship	Relationship then transaction	Relationship and transaction	Transaction
Goal of negotiation	Win concessions	Secure interests of project and mutual relationship	Secure the business opportunity	Win agreement to as many of your positions as possible
Importance of relationship	Strong	Strong	Moderate	Low
Pace of negotiations	Slow process	Slow courtship	Fast	Sprint
Relationship between parties	Formal	Very formal	Formal	Informal
Risk tolerance	Low	Low	High	High
Amount of detail required	Great	Great	Little	Moderate
Degree of meticulousness	High	High	Low	Moderate
Degree of due diligence	High	High	Moderate	High
Negotiation logic	Holistic	Holistic	Holistic	Linear/ straightforward
Communication	Indirect and vague	Indirect and vague	Direct and clear	Direct and clear
Tone	Cautious	Meticulous	Impulsive	Pragmatic, efficient
Use of mediators	Strong	Strong	Moderate	Weak
Prevalence of posturing	Strong	Weak	Moderate	Strong
Legal status of using bribes	Forbidden	Forbidden	Forbidden	Forbidden
Actual use of bribes	Commonplace	Unusual	Occasional	Rare
Agreement content	Detailed & fluid	General & fixed	General & fluid	Highly detailed & fixed

Trait	China	Japan	Korea	America
Degree of legal recourse in commercial dispute	Low	High	Moderate	High
Common means of resolving disputes	Third party intermediary	Good faith face-to-face discussions, intermediary	Good faith face-to-face discussions, then intermediary	Legal action
Time horizon in negotiating	Long term	Long term	Midterm	Short term
Respect for/protection of intellectual property	Weak	Strong	Moderate	Strong
Prominence of fanfare	Extreme	Weak	Moderate	Weak
Role of ritual	Moderate	Strong	Weak	Weak
Use of silence	Strong	Strong	Weak	Weak
Preferred type of eye contact	Indirect and intermittent	Indirect and intermittent	Direct	Direct and continuous
Decision-making style	Highest ranking executive	Group consensus	Group	Highest ranking executive
Speed of decision making	Very slow	Very slow	Very fast	Fast
Comfort with change	Moderate	Weak	Weak	Strong

Source: Robert Charles Azar

CHAPTER 3

NEGOTIATION PROTOCOLS

I. APPROPRIATE VENUE AND TYPE OF COMMUNICATION

Due in part to the prominence of relationship in business, Asian companies prefer face-to-face meetings rather than telephone or electronic communication such as email and Skype. This is especially true for discussions of substantive matters. In the case of negotiating, face-to-face is imperative. Since relationship building is such an integral part of negotiation in Asia, face-to-face meetings are essential.

Americans place high priority on expediency and convenience. We are comfortable communicating via email and even using email in negotiating. Asians, in contrast, see taking the time, expense, and effort to travel in order to meet face-to-face as a reflection of how important the matter is to them as well as a measure of a company's level of interest and relationship sincerity.

Typically, the frequency of face-to-face communication is the greatest during the early stages of collaboration, starting with the "becoming acquainted" stage and on through the negotiation process, the signing of the business agreement, the official launch of the project, and an appropriate lead-in time. After that, the frequency of face-to-face meetings may decrease, though they still remain an essential part of maintaining both your business interest and your relationship with your Asian partner. This is true for as long as you engage in business together.

After a meaningful amount of time elapses from the time the companies execute a business agreement, begin working together, and are building a successful track record and rapport, Asian executives then have a sufficient comfort level to utilize electronic conferencing such as GoToMeeting and Skype. Younger and more internationally minded managers tend to be the first in their companies to shift to this alternative mode of communication. However, it is worth reiterating that while companies are in the negotiation phase, substantive communication needs to occur in person.

Asian executives will continue to require face-to-face communication even after your business has started in their market in the event of major developments or problems. Examples of these circumstances would include:

- **Regulatory issues:** When your product being sold experiences regulatory problems or questioning

- **Consumer use problems:** In the event harm comes to a customer as a result of using your product

- **Problems with third parties in Asia:** On occasions when difficulties arise with parties other than your sales partner who are involved in your business

- **New product launches:** On the occasion of the launch of any of your company's new products in the Asian market

There are other times face-to-face communication and meetings are highly recommended after project commencement:

- **Sales training for your Asian business partner:** Sales training will be needed both before and after launching your business in Asia. Any foreign company seeking to maximize its success in Asian markets should plan to provide training in new product developments and sales on a regular basis for the duration of its business efforts there. The more you keep your partner company focused on selling your products, the more they will keep their salespeople and marketing efforts focused on selling your products.

- **Product usage training for product retailers and users:** Sales training is necessary when, for example, you sell medical products to your Asian partner (your customer) who, in turn, sells your products to hospitals or clinics (retailers). The clinic then uses your product to treat their patients (product users).

The training for your retailers (hospitals, clinics, etc.) and product users needs to be done jointly by your company and your Asian sales partner.

It is noteworthy that in Asian business, these types of sales and product trainings are engaged at a much greater frequency and for a greater length of time than in the States. There are additional benefits in doing so beyond the usual of providing your business partners with sufficient information about your products or services. These include the following four benefits:

- Obtaining detailed market feedback first-hand regarding your products and business from business partners, retailers, and product end-users

- Ensuring that all parties involved in your business are not only *fully* informed about it but also are *accurately* informed

- Providing training and education directly by your company to those participating in your business to assure effectiveness and accuracy.

This becomes more relevant and necessary when companies in addition to your partner are involved in developing your business. While your partner may be well informed, it is critically important that their first level sub-distributors are fully and accurately informed as well as any other related parties such as second level sub-distributors, wholesale companies, retail agents, logistics companies, and product spokespersons.

- Retaining the focus of Asian companies involved in your business

  This goes beyond your contract partners and is especially necessary and effective for those local entities that do not directly interact or report to you but who contribute to your company's success. Such parties include sub-distributors, wholesale companies, logistics companies, product spokespersons, and media representatives. Regular trainings by your company develop good will, demonstrate long-term commitment, and directly contribute to building and sustaining momentum for your business in the market.

- Engaging in marketing events that target prospective clients as well as media representatives

Initial negotiating meetings typically take place in Asia. Given the time and expense of traveling to that continent, it is not only fair but also reasonable and appropriate for some of the negotiation meetings to take place in the States. The perfect time for American executives to suggest that the next meeting be in the U.S. is at the conclusion of a meeting in Asia. Inviting the Asian company to meet in America at your U.S. corporate headquarters signals to them that you are serious about wanting to build a strong working relationship with them.

As your company endeavors to engage in business in Asia, it is common for more meetings to take place there than in America as you will want to make firsthand observations and decisions

> If the Asian company hesitates to come to the States for negotiating meetings, that is a major red flag.

about the local market. This might include such actions as visiting factories, warehouses, distributors, and retail sales channels. However, if the Asian company hesitates or does not agree to your invitation to come to the States for negotiating meetings, that is a major red flag. It is a clear sign that their interest in working with your company is weak. It likewise demonstrates an insufficient commitment to your business project. In that case, it would be better to move on and seek another business partner for that market. Accepting or declining to meet at your corporate headquarters may seem a subtle action, but nonetheless, it is one that speaks volumes.

American executives often suggest Hawaii as a location for face-to-face meetings with Asian companies as a sensible way to deal with meeting venue. While Hawaii is a good midpoint location for American-Asian meetings, having negotiating meetings there does not carry the same significance as meeting at your company's corporate headquarters unless, of course, your headquarters is in Hawaii.

Should your U.S. company request an initial negotiating meeting in Hawaii and not at your corporate headquarters, Asian executives will interpret this as a weak interest in them as your partner. They will assume you must be having similar discussions with other potential partners and have not yet narrowed the field. Your proposing a meeting in the U.S. at any venue other than your corporate location also suggests relational distance to a prospective Asian business partner.

When the Asian firm suggests a Hawaii rendezvous instead of initially meeting at your corporate headquarters that likewise is a red flag. They may be more interested in the opportunity to travel to Hawaii to enjoy a few days in the sun and on the golf course than in pursuing business with your company. Asian executives enjoy golf as much as—if not more than—American executives.

Where meetings take place has an additional significance in Asia that is not found in the U.S. Namely, the more important the topic of the discussion, the more "appropriate" the venue must be. This trait is especially strong in the Japanese market.

> The more important the topic of the discussion, the more "appropriate" the venue must be.

Here is an example that demonstrates very clearly cultural pitfalls for the unwary. During a negotiation between an American client company and a Japanese firm, negotiations were going well. The Japanese company was extremely well suited as a partner for the American company, and the American company stood to gain a very valuable business market in Japan. Then right before adjourning for the day to enjoy dinner together, the Japanese company responded they were dedicating twelve of their best salesmen solely to the American product. As everyone was walking to the nearby restaurant, the American sales director suddenly asked his Japanese counterpart how only twelve salesmen could cover the entire Japanese market. Unfortunately, what the American did not know was that it was both a serious breach of protocol and an insult to speak of such a serious matter "on the street." Later that evening I received a phone call from the company's president expressing his firm's anger and disappointment relating to this incident, which almost permanently derailed the negotiations.

It is imperative for American executives to keep in mind that the more important the topic, the more appropriate the venue and time need to be to address it. Waiting on a street corner for a traffic light to change was definitely neither the correct place nor time for a discussion of that significance. The Japanese perceived his attempted street corner conversation as unprofessional and disrespectful, not only to them but to the business project itself.

Here are common times and places that are appropriate to discuss topics important to you and your Asian partner:

- During official business meetings at the offices or facilities of either company

- A formal meeting room in a hotel

- During a meal at a restaurant

- In the evening over dinner or drinks

- On the golf course

Places where substantive business subjects are never discussed include:

- In hallways

- In elevators

- On the street

- In taxis

- In rest rooms

- In the lobby of a hotel or company offices

- While walking

It is important to remember that Asians are much more formal and have a stronger notion of propriety than Americans tend to have. In their culture, there is an appropriate time, place, and way to conduct meetings and discuss matters. Abiding by those "appropriate" ways is how respect is shown to the other party. Following the prescribed protocol is how each party demonstrates its level of interest in the mutual relationship and business. It is how harmony is promoted. And it is how misunderstanding and friction are avoided in Asian societies.

II. COUNTER-PROPOSING AND SAYING NO

Another fundamental negotiating protocol in Asia is what to say and, more importantly, what *not* to say. In Asian negotiating, saying "no" or directly disagreeing is not typically done. There are two major reasons for this.

The first reason is that saying "no" or directly disagreeing is impolite and is related to the broader cultural

> Another fundamental negotiating protocol in Asia is what to say and, more importantly, what not to say.

orientation in Asia of valuing respect and social harmony. As you will read in chapter four of this book, Asians go to great lengths to avoid being too clear or direct when communicating. Keeping things vague and not saying "no" prevents parties from having to either agree or disagree and thereby take sides. This helps support and promote the cohesion of the group. Consequently, keeping things vague (*aimai ni suru* 曖昧にする in the Japanese language) is a common practice in the art of communication throughout Asian societies. This applies in negotiating as well.

Second, saying no or disagreeing directly indicates you are not concerned about your partner's interests. While that approach is acceptable in American distributive and integrative negotiating as discussed in chapter one, it is not in Asian markets. By saying "no" you are not only rejecting the specific idea proposed but you also are rejecting outright the larger corporate interest your partner is attempting to discuss with you. In the Asian business cultural context, this makes you appear inflexible and demonstrates that you are not negotiating with "sincerity" or what would be termed as in good faith in American culture.

How then can American executives, speaking in English, say "no" or disagree without offending their potential business partners in cultures that avoid saying "no"? In mediating between Asian and American cultures and languages, I have found two methods that work very well for Americans to disagree in a culturally appropriate manner.

The first option is instead of replying with "no," respond with "That might be difficult." This generally translates well into the local culture. While you are not saying no, you are saying you are not in a position to agree, at least not at this point in time, but may be able to in the future. With this reply, you do not come across as being inflexible or disinterested in the interests of the other party but neither have you committed to anything. Also, you have left open the possibility that agreement might be possible at a later point.

The second way to indicate politely that your answer is "no" without alienating the Asian company is to reply with a counterproposal. In other words, if an Asian company is proposing a point that you cannot agree to, do not reply about that point. Instead answer by saying, "That certainly is one option for achieving that, but would another option be XYZ?" Then go on to describe your counterproposal.

This communication tactic serves U.S. executives well in the following five ways which are explained in depth in chapter four:

- Allows you to say no in a culturally acceptable manner

- Helps your Asian counterparts win agreement within their own company to your counterproposal

- Further advances your business interests

- Allows you come across as a being an open-minded firm that takes the other company's interests into account

- Demonstrates in the negotiation that your company is a desirable potential business partner

This cultural dynamic of promoting social harmony through vague and indirect communication carries such importance that Asians have socially acceptable methods to disagree and numerous expressions to use to convey "no," most of which a Westerner would not recognize as dissent or disagreement.

Let's look at one interesting, socially acceptable method to convey dissent. There is the opportunity to say "no" through a trusted third party. Asians may be vague and non-committal during a meeting or even reply to proposals saying "yes," then have a third party directly convey their non-agreement after the meeting. The use of third parties in business negotiations is widespread to avoid direct disagreement or conflict, thereby maintaining good relations (harmony) between the parties, Asian to Asian as well as Asian to foreign.

Western executives, however, often take this communication dynamic to mean that the Asians were not being forthright. This, however, is not the case. The motivation in using this dynamic is actually to demonstrate respect and signal their continued interest in working with your company. While so many Asian communication dynamics are misunderstood as being unfavorable or negative by foreigners negotiating in Asia, in reality they are positive. The most effective ways I have found for navigating this chronic challenge are presented in chapters four and five.

When Asians do dissent face-to-face, the plethora of expressions they can use come into play. I know of twenty-two ways to say "no" in the Japanese language. So many options indicate just how important it is to avoid replying "no" directly and illustrate how many ways the culture provides for accommodating this preference with nuanced phrases.

Of these twenty-two ways to signal "no," many are either non-committal or are even outright positive in their literal meaning. For example, the word *chotto* (ちょっと) literally means "a little." It is a very good example of a word that is non-committal in that the literal meaning indicates neither agreement nor disagreement. However, when used as a reply to a proposal or request, it is universally understood in Japan to mean a clear "no." It can be used as a single word or in the phrase *Sore wa chotto* (それはちょっと), which literally means "that is a little." Despite it being a very vague phrase in its literal meaning, its actual meaning is crystal clear culturally—definitely "no"!

> Of these twenty-two ways to signal "no," many are either non-committal or are even outright positive in their literal meaning.

It is interesting to note that in the ways to disagree you will find not only the word "no" but also the word "yes"! That is correct, the word "yes" can also mean "no." This begs certain questions for every Western company conducting business in Japan and other Asian markets: How on track, really, are your understandings with your Asian partners? When they reply "yes," do they really mean "yes"? Do they mean "no"? Do they mean something in between? This communication challenge is analyzed in chapters four and five and includes a list of phrases that culturally signify "no" in the Japanese culture.

> In the ways to disagree you will find not only the word "no" but also the word "yes"!

What other impact does this cultural dynamic have on negotiating in Asia?

U.S. companies almost always rely on their Asian counterparts to provide the translator when meeting. This puts Americans at a great tactical and strategic disadvantage. This point cannot be stressed enough. Because of Asia's code of respect, foreigners only receive polite, literal translations. To understand the actual—that is, cultural—meaning, foreigners must have a translator *on their team* who is in a position to provide accurate cultural interpretation, including being clear when the Asian company is disagreeing with the American company's position. We will pursue this critically important point in detail in chapter five.

> The difference between the literal meaning and the actual cultural meaning is socially sanctioned in Asia.

Looking past the negotiation stage, Asian cultural and communication dynamics can easily lead to inaccurate communication and misunderstandings throughout the entire period of working together. Keep in mind that the difference between the literal meaning and the actual cultural meaning is socially sanctioned in Asia. For example, so well established is this communication dynamic that in Japan it is codified in the notion of *tatemae* (建前) and *honne* (本音)—that is, what is ostensibly the case versus what is the actual situation. This important communication dynamic of *tatemae* and *honne* is examined in chapter four.

III. INDICATORS OF INTEREST DURING NEGOTIATIONS

As we have seen, negotiating in Asia requires a greater

amount of time and input than in the U.S., so how can American executives gauge the level of interest their Asian counterparts have in working together as the negotiation progresses? There are actions that are positive interest level indicators, and there are red flags to be mindful of as well. These next sections shed light on how foreign executives can better read where Asian executives stand during negotiations.

A.   WHO ATTENDS THE NEGOTIATION MEETINGS

The first indicator Asian companies give of their level of interest in your business is who is representing them in the early discussions and negotiations. Here are five specific signs that American executives can look for in this regard:

- **Rank of attendees:** How senior in the company are the participants? High-level executives attending represent a high level of interest. Conversely, junior manager or third-party representatives are indicative of weaker or uncertain interest.

- **Number of attendees:** How many individuals are attending the negotiation meetings? Two or three representatives? Or, on the other hand, six or seven? The greater the number of representatives attending, the greater the interest their company has in doing business with you.

  By way of example, the greatest number of individuals representing an Asian firm in a negotiation that I have experienced is fourteen. That included the company CEO, senior executives, the heads of all of the departments that would be involved in the business, top salesmen, and the CEO's executive assistant. When the two executives of my American client and I entered the meeting room and saw them all standing behind their chairs at the board room conference table, there was no doubt about the seriousness of their interest in our business.

Conversely, U.S. companies typically send fewer representatives—often one or two. While this makes sense from an efficiency standpoint, it is important to keep in mind the cultural significance that can be read into this in Asia. This is one instance where it is recommended to avoid being penny-wise and pound-foolish. Demonstrate the importance of the business negotiation to your company with a greater investment in who and how many you send to represent you.

- **Number of departments:** The number of departments in the Asian company represented at the negotiating table is another good indicator of level of interest. The greater the company's interest, the greater the number of departments that will want to participate. There are two reasons for this.

First, pursuant to the Asian group style of decision-making discussed earlier, all departments that will be involved in a new business endeavor actively participate in deciding whether or not the company should embark on the new business project. To make an informed decision, they need to be involved beginning with the early discussions and negotiations.

Second, given that these various departments will be directly responsible for executing the business, they want to be as knowledgeable about it as possible, as early as possible in the process, so they can be best prepared.

Given these circumstances, the number of departments represented in negotiations is a solid indicator of how serious an Asian company's interest is in your business.

- **Number and locations of major regional offices represented:** For example, in China are all of the attendees from Beijing only? Or are the heads of the company's major regional locations present as well, such as Shanghai, Guangzhou, Chengdu, and Shenzhen. The same reasons for the number of departments apply to the number of major regional offices represented.

In addition, attendees from major regional offices signal that the Asian company sees your business in their market as being nationwide, not limited to a few major cities. It also suggests the ability to engage in your business on a nationwide basis. Such major regional offices in Japan would include Osaka, Nagoya, Shizuoka, and Fukuoka. In Korea, they are Pusan, Incheon, and Daegu.

I strongly recommend American executives inquire during the negotiation how the prospective Asian partner's way of engaging in your business might vary between the capital city and other regional areas. Sometimes differences are warranted due to the differing business circumstances in various parts of their country. Those do not generally represent a concern for a U.S. company. However, I have often found that the execution of a client's business varied in geographical areas for reasons that are problematic and American executives need to be aware of such circumstances early on in the negotiations.

For example, while claiming in the negotiations to be able to provide you with full, nationwide coverage of their market, regional inconsistencies in execution of your business can reveal that their actual presence and ability in those geographic locations is weak and, therefore, troublesome. American executives may decide to remove that company from further consideration as a result.

Another circumstance I have come across is that while an Asian company may have a regional location outside the capital city, the location is not appropriate or beneficial for the specific needs of your business in that market.

- **Seating arrangement of attendees:** Asians typically sit in one of two formations in negotiating meetings.

The first seating order is hierarchical with the senior most executive seated in the middle on his company's side of the table and the others seated on either side of him in descending rank within the company, similar to the placement of the pieces in the game of chess. Those sitting at the ends of the table will be the lowest ranking members of the company on the Asian side of the meeting table. This hierarchical seating order means your discussions are proceeding smoothly, and they are on board with your business so far.

The second order is the departmental seating arrangement with the senior executive sitting in the middle but the other representatives are sitting grouped by their departments. This seating arrangement means that they have questions or points that they need to clarify before moving forward with the negotiations. Therefore, expect them to raise questions or points to go over in greater detail. They may opt to discuss your replies among their departments right then and there to ensure accuracy of understanding and allow for immediate and additional follow-up questions or clarifications. While this negotiating dynamic may add to the length of the negotiation, it is favorable because it demonstrates genuine and serious interest in your business.

B. FREQUENCY OF NEGOTIATION MEETINGS

The request for follow-up negotiation meetings is another indicator of Asian interest in your business, both when the request for the next meeting is made and for how far in the future the follow-up meeting is requested. Two weeks between rounds of negotiating is a good rule of thumb to keep in mind. Barring a special circumstance or event, if an Asian company does not want to meet within two weeks of concluding a round of negotiation meetings that generally is a sign they have limited interest—a definite red flag for foreign executives.

> Two weeks between rounds of negotiating is a good rule of thumb to keep in mind.

Likewise, a request by the Asian company for a follow-up meeting during a current meeting is an indicator of stronger interest than if the request comes after the current meeting has already concluded and the foreign executives have returned to their country.

C. LENGTH OF NEGOTIATING MEETINGS

In some international markets, the length of a meeting is indicative of the level of interest in what is being discussed. This is certainly true in Asia. When Asian executives meet with you for one or two hours, their interest level is still not strong; meeting for four or more hours in one day shows good interest. When an Asian company wants to meet with you for two full days or more, that is a sign of very serious interest in your business. By way of illustration, the longest negotiating session I have experienced in Asia is three-and-a-half days of back-to-back, all-day meetings.

D. LEVEL OF COMPANY RESOURCES COMMITTED

Given the Asian penchant for taking a long-term view of business, the amount of corporate resources they state in the negotiation that they will commit to your business over time is a solid indicator of how seriously they view your business and their role in it. This includes not only the size and scope of their marketing and sales plan and the attending budget but also the size of the sales team they would utilize, the number of locations throughout their market, whether they will market and sell the products just through their own company or utilize sub-distributors and partners, and, if applicable, the number of sales channels they will sell in.

IV. GIFT GIVING

> Gifts are also a token of appreciation for the mutual business relationship.

Exchanging gifts has long been a part of doing business in Asia. Doing so is not only a means to build good will as in the States but is also an expression of gratitude for the opportunity to work together. Gifts are also a token of appreciation for the mutual business relationship.

Foreigners are often confused about the gift giving protocol, particularly how often and on what occasions gifts should be exchanged. For example, do they have to be exchanged at every meeting for as long as the companies engage in negotiations or business together?

Commonly, gifts are exchanged at the first negotiation

meeting that takes place in Asia as well as the first that occurs in the U.S. or other location outside Asia. I always recommend a third gift exchange on the occasion of the successful completion of negotiating and signing of the mutual business agreement. Once engaged in business together, gifts are typically no longer exchanged at a set frequency but rather periodically. For example, gifts might be exchanged during meetings to celebrate the achieving of major milestones in the business project. It is also recommended that U.S. companies send their Asian partners New Year's greeting cards every year.

As you might expect by now, there are things to consider when choosing a gift to present. Here are two basic categories of gifts that work well:

- **Emblematic to your company**: Consider gifting an item specific and emblematic to your company. For example, one of your products either mounted or in a case, if they are of appropriate scale, could make a good gift. A jet engine obviously would not work, but a semiconductor chip in a display case would. Being incased in a display case is necessary if your product is a part and not a finished product. Presentation is important. In the event your company produces perishable products, a small replica of your product would be an appropriate gift. For instance, if you manufacture ice cream, a small model of your ice cream perhaps in a cone in a display stand. Another option would be a high-end item that has your company name or corporate logo or both on it.

- **General gifts:** Items unrelated to your firm or business are in the second category. These can include both high and lower-end products. An example of a high-end gift would be a crystal vase, while a lower-end product would be a basket of special jams and preserves produced in the state where your corporate headquarters is located. One of my favorite gifts to present is a Mont Blanc pen. Highly appreciated by Asian executives, the pens are prestigious, yet not expensive and, given their small size, convenient for carrying with you.

While in the States it is popular to present a framed inspirational quote featuring something like a dramatic nature scene, an athlete conquering the heights of a mountain, or a crew navigating their boat in a race that can be hung on a wall, it is important to remember that in Asia it is not common to decorate office walls with anything other than calendars. So, such items would not be appropriate for a gift to an Asian executive. Instead, small items that can be placed on a desk work well.

It is also advisable to avoid items that are size specific. For example, the letter size paper we use in the States is not used in Asia. Instead, they use A4 size paper. Accordingly, a beautiful leather portfolio for an American 8½ by 11 inch note pad would not be an appropriate gift as their A4 size pad will not fit. It is well known how prevalent business cards are in conducting business in Asia, the significance of which is analyzed in chapter four of this book. However, the size of business cards in Asia is different than in America—larger actually. Therefore, leather business card holders and cases are also not appropriate gift items. Since the countries of Asia use the metric system in measuring, not the U.S. system, avoiding size specific items is advisable.

Other gift-giving considerations include the color and number of the items. While black is viewed as a sophisticated and high-end color in America, it is to be avoided at all costs in Asia as it is widely associated with funerals. In the same way, the number four is to be avoided in Asia as it is associated with death in those countries that use Chinese characters because the pronunciation of the words four and death are very similar in some Asian languages. Also noteworthy regarding quantity in gifts is that in America, a gift containing more than one piece such as crystal wine glasses or coasters is generally packaged with an even number of pieces—four, six, eight, or twelve. In Asia, gifts only come with an odd number of items, typically three or five. So, while the gift an American executive might prepare will contain half a dozen items in one gift, your Asian counterpart's gift to you is likely to contain five items. No need to feel you were shortchanged by this cultural difference!

> Other gift-giving considerations include the color and number of the items.

Finally, the common practice is for each company to present just one gift to the company they are meeting with, regardless of how many individuals from each firm might actually be attending. This eliminates the worry about having enough gifts—it is one gift per company. This reinforces the notion explained in chapter two that in most Asian markets negotiating takes place organization to organization, not individual to individual. The gift is given to the senior representative of each company attending the negotiating meeting. It is common that the senior executive of the Asian company does not present his company's gift himself. Instead a junior executive will present the gift. When small- and medium-sized companies exchange gifts, the presidents or other highest-ranking executive may present the gifts themselves. It is advisable for American executives to follow the same protocol.

V. MEETING AGENDAS

In most Asian markets, agendas are necessary for all meetings and discussions, and they must be provided in advance of the meeting. If an agenda is not provided, Asian executives will consider it unprofessional of you.

Asians do not like surprises; being caught by surprise results in losing face. Also, it would be rude of them not to be able to reply to a query that might arise in the meeting. They want to know in advance what will be discussed at the meeting so they can be properly prepared. Also, keep in mind that, as mentioned earlier and as will be discussed in chapter four, Asians are put in an awkward position if they have to say "no." Being able to review the agenda before the meeting allows them to ascertain how they can best discuss your topics and that allows them to feel comfortable and in control regarding the meeting. Asian executives want to be professional as well as prepared to deal with your topics in a meaningful way.

Americans sometimes feel locked in by the pre-established meeting topics provided by Asian companies. To avoid this and allow for flexibility regarding the topics discussed in the meeting, I recommend always adding "Other" as the last topic on the agenda. This will help American executives maximize the value of the meeting without violating the Asian custom of following agenda topics.

In addition to an agenda, it is also a good business practice to send along a brief profile for each attendee on your team ahead of meetings. Adding an accompanying headshot is highly recommended. This is helpful and appreciated by the Asian company as it will assist the Asian negotiating team in understanding each attendee's name and role in your company. This is especially helpful for those Asians who do not speak English and would otherwise stumble through the initial introductions and name card exchanges with your team only to remain in the dark about with whom they are interacting. As you can imagine, that is not an ideal situation in cultures where establishing a relationship has great significance and showing proper respect is important.

> Providing these three things in advance goes a long way toward getting your negotiation off to a favorable start.

Providing these three things in advance—the meeting agenda, brief profiles describing each person's role, and a headshot for each U.S. team member—goes a long way toward getting your negotiation and prospective relationship off to a favorable start.

VI. REGIONAL AND HISTORICAL CONSIDERATIONS

Companies in America can, for the most part, engage in business across the entire nation in a consistent manner. This is the result of our language, business practices, and other factors being relatively uniform. Despite the U.S. market extending from one side of an entire continent to the other, companies can conduct business seamlessly in this geographical arena. This is not true in many Asian countries.

China and Japan, for example, are made up of dozens of provinces (or prefectures), autonomous regions, municipality areas, and special administrative regions. Within each country, there are multiple differences in regional languages, business practices, distribution systems, and the like. These variations often present challenges to American executives negotiating and conducting business in those markets.

> Companies in America can conduct business seamlessly. This is not true in many Asian countries.

For example, nationwide marketing, distribution, and sales are usually readily available and commonplace in America. Manufacturers expect one company to be able to get their products on retail shelves and in showrooms from coast to coast, utilizing distribution companies, sales companies, or a combination of both to get access to nationwide capability.

In contrast, while nationwide marketing, distribution, and sales are, of course, present in China, Japan, and Korea, they are not always achieved in the direct, straightforward manner, or to the same extent they are in the U.S. Instead, marketing, distribution, and sales can be highly fragmented into regional and even local distribution networks. This may require putting in place a network of different regional or local companies to execute nationwide sales. As a result, product marketing, distribution, and sales can require negotiating with several sales companies and be more cumbersome, costly, and time consuming than in the States. These added layers contribute to the higher retail price-to-production cost ratio common for many products in the Japanese market.*

Efforts by American firms to put in place nationwide sales and distribution are complicated—and often simply precluded— by the fact that the local sales and distribution systems operate based on decades old relationships which foreign companies do not have. It is not unusual in Asian markets for sales companies in their nation's capital to be unable to sell directly in local provinces since they lack the requisite relationships with local companies. They need to have developed ties with sub-distributors in those local areas to be able to have access to sell there. American companies need to discuss fully and clarify the sales and distribution capabilities of the Asian company during the negotiating process. For major parts of the market outside of the capital region, it is advisable for U.S. executives to take the time to visit the sub-distributors that would be utilized there to handle your business and engage in proper due diligence. Foreign companies that neglect to do so can pay a terrible price down the road.

In the event an Asian company does not maintain a sufficient network of sub-distributors throughout their market, fragmented sales and distribution systems and the need for local business relationships may necessitate U.S. companies negotiate with more than one business partner in order to achieve nationwide sales and distribution and full market penetration in an Asian country.

---

* For more information on this aspect of product sales and distribution in Japan, see Robert Charles Azar, *Navigating Japan's Business Culture* (Raleigh, NC: Write Way Publishing Co., 2016) chapters four, six, and eight.

In Korea, I was surprised to experience how small- and medium-sized companies in Seoul and throughout the country often do not conduct business with firms in other parts of country. This is a remnant of the centuries-old rivalry between the three kingdoms that comprised Korea throughout most of its history (Shilla, Paekche, and Koryeo). As a result, engaging in business outside of one's geographic region and on a national scale requires a company to set up its own subsidiaries in different parts of the country. As this scaling is beyond the ability of many small- and medium-sized firms, this regional dynamic is one of the factors that contributes to Korea's four major conglomerates dominating eighty percent of the entire nation's economy today.

U.S. executives need to be aware of this history-based business condition and clarify during their discussions with Korean companies their actual capabilities in providing comprehensive countrywide market coverage. This situation may necessitate U.S. companies negotiating with more than one business partner in order to achieve nationwide sales and distribution and full market penetration there.

Another historical consideration American executives would benefit from keeping in mind is what languages are used when negotiating in different Asian markets.

Another historical consideration American executives would benefit from keeping in mind is what languages are used when negotiating in different Asian markets. Allow me to cite an example.

I was living in Seoul at the time and maintained an office for my management consulting firm in the high end Kangnam section of town. The business professional who worked with me as my righthand man, Mr. Nam, was a native Korean who spoke no English. I speak only rudimentary Korean. However, he had worked in Osaka for six years and was a fluent speaker of Japanese. As that was the language we shared in common, we communicated exclusively in Japanese. During a negotiation meeting with the president and other senior executives of a Seoul-based Korean company where none of the executives spoke English, I had the following experience.

We were seated on opposite sides of a long but narrow table that was no more than three feet wide. About five minutes into the meeting, the Korean company president sitting directly opposite me suddenly stood up, leaned forward toward me, and, grabbing my necktie, pulled me up so he and I were literally standing nose to nose over the table. He then began to yell at me in Korean.

While I could not understand what he was saying, the vehemence and anger behind his words needed no translation. Meanwhile, out of the corner of my eye, I could see that Mr. Nam was shocked and squirming in his seat. With sweat beginning to appear on his face, he began to translate into Japanese for me. Editing out the foul language of the Korean company president, his message went along the following lines:

How DARE you speak that god-forsaken language in this country! Don't you know where you are? Don't you know the history between Korea and THAT country?

This company president was articulating the ill will toward Japan that can be found in Korea even today, a consequence of the history between those two countries. It is important to know how the language that you and your translator speak in negotiations can impact the other parties.

Both the role and the influence of language and regional language differences are discussed further in chapter four.

VII. OTHER BUSINESS PRACTICE PROTOCOLS

A. DINING AND DRINKING

Sharing a meal as a means to build rapport is common in most countries, and Asia is no exception. Dining provides an opportunity to step outside of the formal atmosphere of the negotiation and interact with your counterparts in a more relaxed and personal manner. It is an occasion to develop a greater familiarity and comfort level that contributes to the mutual business relationship of the parties involved.

Comparing China, Japan, and Korea, dining plays the greatest role in China where companies raise the typical business dinner to a new level and lavish complete banquets on foreign executives. Once working together with a track record of success, Chinese companies often invite local dignitaries such as the town mayor to the banquets. This fanfare is done for the sake of relationship building and impressing foreign companies. While dining is equally important in Japan and Korea, it is not engaged in at the lavish level found in China.

A key part of relationship building through business dining is drinking. It is seen as the opportunity for the members of both parties to show their true personalities. This is especially true in China and Korea. As a customary saying in China explains:

The truth about oneself comes out when you drink. — (jiu hou tu zhen yan 酒后吐真言)

> In Korea, drinking is often turned into a duel as Korean executives seek to see "what you are made of."

As is true in other aspects of business, propriety and ritual play a role in drinking in China, Japan, and Korea where it is polite for the members of company A to pour the drinks of those in company B, and vice versa. In China and Korea, you may pour your own drink but only last. In Japan, individuals never pour their own, unless they are at the bottom on the hierarchical totem pole present at that time. In Korea, American businessmen and women need to be aware that drinking is often turned into a duel as Korean executives seek to see "what you are made of."

Allow me to share my first experience with this. I was the sole representative of my client and having dinner with eight executives of the Korean company I had just concluded meetings with on behalf of my client. We began drinking by everyone toasting with a shot of whiskey. As soon we finished that, the president of the Korean company handed his empty shot glass to me, filled it up as I held it, and looked at me with a huge grin. It was clear that he was waiting for me to down that shot and return his glass to him. I did so and then filled his glass. Great, I thought. That's the end of that. Well, not quite.

Next the executive vice president of the company handed me his empty shot glass, filled it as I held it, and waited for me to return it to him empty so he could enjoy another. And so on with each of the remaining six company executives, going in order of their seniority in the company. So, by the time each of them finished their second shot, I had had nine. It was clear I was in the middle of a drinking fest, and the Koreans did not waste time in catching up! What is the goal in this ritual? To allow executives from both companies to see each other's true colors.

It is not uncommon for these drinking marathons in Korea to end with executives being so under the influence that they cannot even get up. Restaurant owners and staff are accustomed to putting them in taxi cabs to send them to their homes or nearby hotels. While I still had my wits about me, I did need a helping hand to hail a taxi to return to my hotel that night.

Over time I came to realize that these drinking contests were not just to test my mettle. They were also an opportunity for the Koreans to de-stress and let off steam, to build camaraderie and to promote esprit de corps. While that may work for local executives, U.S. executives who have traveled to Korea need to keep in mind that this drinking experience on top of jet lag and the fatigue of the long journey can impair their ability to be effective in business the next day. This is especially true if you are negotiating with more than one company during the same trip to a country and have to deal with this protocol with each of them on different evenings. It is important to realize that when your Asian counterpart holds a bottle wanting to fill your glass, they do not accept no for an answer. This is one instance where Asians do not hesitate to directly disagree!

How can U.S. executives effectively deal with this business protocol? One method I discovered is to turn my glass upside down immediately upon sitting down for dinner and notify my Korean counterparts that I am not able to drink for medical reasons. While they are visibly disappointed upon hearing that, it is understood and accepted. The key is to smoothly and quickly encourage them to enjoy their beverages while you have a non-alcoholic drink.

VIII. PROBLEMATIC BUSINESS PRACTICES

A. BRIBERY

Bribery is illegal in China, Japan, and Korea. While officially banned in all three markets, American executives need to be aware that it is practiced to differing degrees in those countries.

Outright prohibited in China; bribery nonetheless is part of conducting business there. The common understanding is that the government will look the other way when company executives engage in bribery but crack down on government officials who engage in it. However, I can recount numerous times when I was expected to pay a bribe to government officials in order to advance client projects.

In one case, I was meeting with the head of one of China's ministries in the early years of my doing business there to discuss the approval process of a client's products so they could be imported and sold. After showing the minister the ingredient list (names only), I inquired if any of the ingredients were problematic in receiving government approval. He spoke for five minutes in reply but provided no indication, saying it could go either way. I asked the same question later in the conversation, only to get the same result. I later repeated the same inquiry for a third time and likewise received only a non-committal answer.

In every other Asian market where I had the same discussion with the head of the comparable ministry, I was immediately provided with a definitive response. Baffled by the outcome in China, I spoke to my native Chinese associate, Mr. Chen, who had accompanied me to the meeting and had translated for me about this. He replied:

> *"Robert, don't you understand? When a decision-maker in China gives a vague answer when in fact he knows the answer that means he expects you to give him money under the table. This is business in China."*

B. INACCURATE DOCUMENTS

Another practice U.S. companies need to be aware of is that documents provided by the company you are negotiating with in China may not be the complete document. Or the translations of documents may intentionally be inaccurate and some information may not be included so as to put a foreign company at a disadvantage in negotiations. This is discussed in detail in chapter five, but the point is, it is imperative that American executives have a native speaker on their team who can verify the accuracy and entirety of documents exchanged during negotiating meetings.

INSIGHTS

In this chapter, we examined how the protocols involved in Asian negotiation differ so vastly from those we are accustomed to in the States. Major protocols covered include the following ten items:

- Appropriate venues for negotiating

- Types of communication required

- Frequency of communication

- Saying no and counter-proposing

- Understanding the indicators of interest and non-interest

- Gift giving

- Meeting agenda content

- Regional and historical factors that impact Asian negotiating

- Dining and drinking

- Problematic business practices to be aware of when negotiating in Asia

Being aware of differing negotiation protocols enables you to properly prepare for them and remove them as obstacles to your success. In addition, once aware of these differences, you will be able to leverage them to better advance your corporate interests.

PART TWO

CRITICAL ROLE OF COMMUNICATION

CHAPTER 4

COMMUNICATION DYNAMICS:

The Stealth Determinant

"He who knows does not speak. He who speaks does not know." — **Lao-Tsu**[*]

"The single biggest problem in communication is the illusion that it has taken place." — **George Bernard Shaw**

I. ROLE AND IMPACT IN NEGOTIATION

Communication plays a critical role in negotiating. It is the very lifeline of negotiating. Its presence, role, importance, and influence cannot be emphasized enough. When negotiating

---

[*] Lao-Tsu was the prominent sixth century BC Chinese philosopher who authored the *Tao Te Ching*. This book became the foundation of Taoism, a philosophy that has dominated much of Asia ever since.

internationally, especially interculturally, its import and impact are even greater. Specifically, communication impacts negotiations in the following ways:

- Communication is the vehicle through which parties negotiate.

- Proper communication enables accuracy in message content delivery—linking what is said to what is meant to be conveyed. This factor is even more critical when parties negotiate through a translator and across cultures.

- Good communication is one of the major determinants of how timely, smoothly, and effectively the negotiation proceeds.

- Clear communication is one of the major determinants of how successful companies are in obtaining their negotiating objectives.

> Despite its profound significance in negotiating, communication receives nowhere near the attention or preparation it warrants.

Despite its profound significance in negotiating, however, communication receives nowhere near the attention or preparation it warrants. In my experience, communication is one facet of a negotiation that is almost always overlooked by companies as they prepare for, engage in, subsequently reflect back on, and strategize negotiation follow up. The result is never positive.

In the context of international negotiating—more accurately, intercultural negotiating—unfavorable consequences are almost assured. Specifically, the challenge is that, unaware of the ramification of communication, companies do not include communication considerations *in their preparations* for negotiations, do not recognize the impact of communication *during negotiations*, and are unaware of how to deal with or rectify any negative consequences of communication dynamics *after each negotiating session concludes*. In this way, communication dynamics are the stealth determinant of negotiating.

> The degree of accuracy of understanding in U.S.-Asian negotiating is approximately seventy to ninety percent.

One of the most fundamental areas of impact is the degree of accuracy of understanding in U.S.-Asian negotiating. In my experience, the average level of accuracy of understanding between American companies engaging in negotiations in Asia is approximately seventy to ninety percent. I know this as I have translated negotiations and other business discussions between American and European client companies in Japan for nearly four decades. When it was not my role to translate, I would nonetheless need to interject and either fill in the missing ten to thirty percent or outright correct the translation provided by the interpreters of the Japanese firm. Insufficient accuracy is also common in formal presentations such as those at company training programs, conferences, and trade shows.

This problem of insufficient accuracy or outright

incorrectness occurs not only regarding the facts and figures discussed but more significantly it also applies to the strategies, objectives, expectations, and intentions of the parties involved in negotiating. It is one of the most profound and ever-present potential deal breakers of every international negotiation and resulting business venture. In this chapter and the next, we will analyze this topic in detail.

When business executives sit down at the negotiating table, they bring with them the communication dynamics and the cultural norms from their own country and culture. These dynamics and norms include the cultural connotations, nuances, sensibilities, assumptions, and expectations that the hearer attaches to what is said, heard, understood, reflected upon, experienced, replied to, and executed.

In America, for example, we prefer communication to be direct and clear, succinct and definitive. We prefer either yes or no answers and I agree or I disagree statements. In our culture, directness and clarity are seen favorably to reduce miscommunication and promote understanding and progress. Directness, clarity, and thoroughness add confidence that our communication will be effective and ensure that all parties are on the same page. Accordingly, a common three-fold rule of thumb in American presentations is to: (1) tell the audience what you are going to tell them, (2) tell them, and (3) then tell them what you just told them. In other words, as we often say in the vernacular: *Leave no doubt!*

In most Asian markets, this is not the case at all. In fact, very different social values and cultural dynamics inform communication and business practices in general there. The result is that effective communication with Asian companies is highly problematic for Westerners and is a major obstacle to attaining business success.

This chapter assesses the profound impact language and communication dynamics have on international negotiating and business. In order to speak from firsthand experience, I have elected to narrow the geographic focus of this chapter to Japan and the Japanese language as it is a language where I am fully functional. Doing so will allow for an in-depth, first-hand, and more meaningful analysis of this essential but commonly over-looked facet of negotiating.

While this chapter presents a thorough case study exam-ination of Japan, the challenges it addresses are common in international business, regardless of geographic location. Conse-quently, the types of challenges American executives find will be similar from market to market; what will differ will be the spe-cific, esoteric remedies unique to each international market and its underlying culture. Let's get started.

II. DIVERGENT GOALS IN COMMUNICATION

The first challenge is that communication in Japan has a very different goal than in America. In the States, the purpose of communication is to express or share an idea or sentiment as clearly as one can. We are encouraged to do so as logically and convincingly as possible. In fact, in describing a good communicator, we use such terms as easy to understand, clear, articulate, lucid, expressive, unambiguous, convincing, and compelling.

While the function of communication in Japan and other Asian markets is likewise to convey a thought or sentiment, there is an additional underlying goal that is not present in America that governs Japan's communication dynamics. That goal of communication, as we have noted previously, is to promote smooth relationships and group harmony. It does that by fostering a sense of mutual belonging and interdependence. This concept will be important throughout this chapter. In consequence of having different goals and drivers, communication in Japan has very different dynamics and characteristics than what we are accustomed to in the States.

> In consequence of having different goals and drivers, communication in Japan has very different dynamics and characteristics.

We have already seen in chapter three that communication is intentionally vague in Japan and that Japanese go to great lengths to avoid being too direct or clear when communicating. Statements that can be understood in more than one way are frequently used. Keeping communication vague means parties do not have to take sides by agreeing or disagreeing, thereby preserving and promoting group solidarity. As a result, "keeping things vague" (*aimai ni suru* 曖昧 にする) is a common feature of Japanese communication used to promote harmony.

As a result of this common practice of keeping things vague, it is not unusual for business meetings to conclude with the parties wondering what just transpired and unsure as to where things stand. When I initially experienced this practice of intentional vagueness while living in Japan, I thought that my Japanese language skills still had a long way to go. However, I quickly realized I was not the only one who could not figure out the meaning of what was said.

When I would ask Japanese colleagues, they replied that they also had no idea—the conversation was intentionally too vague to offer any clear understanding. When that happens, Japanese understand that they will need a one-on-one follow-up meeting with the other party outside of an official meeting to find out where things stand. This could be because the other party does not agree with what was discussed or is not presently in a position to decide. If the other party does not agree to meet for such a follow up meeting, then it becomes clear that their vagueness was the means to indicate they are no longer interested in further negotiations.

It is much more important in Japan to promote the harmony of the group or harmony between the companies negotiating than to lucidly provide the facts of the matter on the table, present a solution, or express one's thoughts or feelings convincingly or unambiguously as we do in the States. An excellent example of this is seen in how speakers who are considered good communicators in Japan read their audience for the purpose of promoting a sense of mutual agreement and group solidarity.

In the Japanese language, the structure of a sentence is first the subject, followed by the direct object, and finally the verb. Good communicators in Japan are those who are able to say the subject and the direct object and then before concluding the sentence with the verb are able to read the audience reaction. If the audience is displeased with the subject and direct object, the skilled speaker conjugates the verb in negative form to express his or her shared dislike. If the audience seems favorably disposed to the subject and direct object, then the speaker conjugates the verb in positive form expressing agreement with the audience.

For example, after saying "I" followed by "nuclear power," the speaker will observe the reaction of the crowd. If the mood or faces of the audience indicate they are not favorably inclined after hearing "I, nuclear power," the speaker is likely to complete the sentence by using the negative form of the verb so that he says "I, nuclear power, disfavor." In correct English: I disfavor nuclear power.

> The Japanese language provides flexibility in order to promote a sense of everyone being in agreement.

On the other hand, if after saying "I" and "nuclear power," the speaker reads the audience reaction as favorable, he will say "I, nuclear power, favor." In this way, the grammatical structure of the Japanese language allows speakers to read the audience and complete their sentences according to the reaction of those listening. The Japanese language thus provides flexibility in order to promote a sense of everyone being in agreement.

Since a primary objective of communication is promoting harmony and smooth relations, it is not appropriate to directly disagree, contradict, or challenge others in formal business meetings or discussions. This is especially true when parties do not yet have a strong relationship as is generally true of Western companies negotiating in Asia.

Most foreigners are not accustomed to this communication dynamic; for the most part, they do not even know it exists. As a result, while Japanese are seeking to promote a smooth relationship with foreigners through vague communication or an absence of a definitive yes or no reply, foreigners typically misunderstand and interpret it as a lack of interest or believe that the Japanese are being disingenuous in the business discussions. In addition to promoting a harmonious relationship, following customary cultural norms by intentionally being vague is a way Japanese show respect for the party they are speaking with. Foreigners' negative interpretation of this stems from a lack of sufficient cultural understanding and experience, another example of why having a facilitator interpreter on your company's team is indispensable.

III. DIFFERENT AND DIFFICULT LANGUAGES

Another reason communication with Japanese is problematic for U.S. companies is that becoming fluent in the Japanese language is very difficult for foreigners. Linguists say Japanese is one of the most difficult languages for non-natives to learn. Part of the reason for this is that Japanese is so very different from most other languages. It shares similarities with the Korean language like similar grammar, pronunciation of many words, and different ways to conjugate verbs to express politeness. However, Japanese has no similarities with Chinese, other Asian languages, or Western languages.

> Learning by association does not work with Japanese or other Asian languages.

Americans typically study French, Italian, Spanish, or other languages by finding similarities with English. That can be done given the inherent similarities between those romance languages and English. However, Japanese is so different from Western languages that there are no points of comparison or similarities to draw on to help us learn it. Consequently, learning by association does not work with Japanese or other Asian languages. Their degree of difference from English is partly the cause of their degree of difficulty.

We immediately realize this when we encounter the writing system of the Japanese language. The roman letters used in English are also used in the European languages, so we use a shared writing system. This clearly is not the case with Japanese. This language has three writing systems, and each is unrelated to English.

One is the Chinese *kanji* (漢字) characters that Japan imported over a thousand years ago. *Kanji* originated in China and were originally pictorial drawings of the word's meaning. Over the centuries, they evolved into their current form. A person needs to know eighteen hundred *kanji* to be able to read a Japanese newspaper. Most Japanese college graduates know approximately two thousand two hundred *kanji*.

The other two writing systems—called *hiragana* (ひらがな) and *katakana* (カタかナ)—are indigenous. They are phonetic letter systems for writing syllables and sounds just as we find in the English alphabet, and, unlike *kanji*, they have no meaning in and of themselves.

There are forty-six *hiragana* symbols and forty-six *katakana*. These two writing systems do not pose significant difficulty for foreigners to learn. The Chinese *kanji* characters, however, are a different story.

Each *kanji* character has its own meaning that must be memorized. What makes that especially challenging is that each character can have several meanings.

Another difficulty is the degree of complexity of the structure and the number of strokes required to write the *kanji* character. For instance, *kanji* characters can either be simple with only a few strokes or complex with numerous strokes. By way of example, the character 鍵 (*kagi*), meaning a key, has as many as seventeen strokes. Some characters have more than twenty strokes. If the number of strokes is not challenging enough, there is a prescribed order for writing each stroke and each one must be placed in the correct position. Since many characters look similar, deviations in placing the strokes can result in a different character being written, which will create a different word and meaning.

The multiple meanings and numerous brush strokes used in writing *kanji* are not the only difficult aspects of Japanese. Reading Japanese is another equally challenging task. First, there are several different ways to read each *kanji* character, and they all must be memorized. For example, the *kanji* meaning "what" is 何. It has as many as six different ways to read it – *ka, nan, nani, dore, izu(re), and dou(shite)*. As you can see, the different readings are unrelated.

Second, most nouns and verbs are written by combining two or three *kanji* characters. As each character can have several possible ways to be read, the result of combining characters is that the number of possible ways to read any given word can be overwhelming. They cannot be learned by association but must be committed to memory.

I remember how daunting a challenge it was when I

studied the Japanese language as a graduate student at Columbia University. There are four levels of Japanese language instruction in that program, and the attrition rate is usually quite high. In the case of my class, level one Japanese language had sixty-four students. Level two had thirty-two. Level three had twelve students, and level four had six students. Only six out of the original sixty-four students, or about ten percent, made it through all four levels. This ninety percent attrition rate was not just the result of students not registering for the next level at the start of a new academic year. Students would just simply stop coming to class throughout the year. Learning Japanese is extremely demanding. In my case, I had to spend five hours a day, seven days a week just for Japanese language study to complete the program.

Similar challenges are involved in learning other Asian languages as well. Due to the great degree of difficulty for foreigners to learn Asian languages, there are few foreigners who can speak them sufficiently well to negotiate or otherwise conduct business in those languages. Consequently, American companies frequently depend on the Asian company to provide a translator. However, this reliance is a major strategic as well as tactical disadvantage for American companies as discussed in chapter five of this book.

IV. HIGHLY INTUITIVE COMMUNICATION

Anthropologists refer to cultures where fewer words are needed to communicate as "high context cultures." That means that the degree of importance of knowing the context of what is being communicated in order to facilitate understanding is high. Phrases such as "reading between the lines" or "reading the tea leaves" apply to high context cultures. Japan is certainly a high context culture. In contrast, English is at the opposite end of the high-low context culture spectrum. As a low context culture, American communication requires thoughts to be expressed fully and clearly in words, without vagueness, so that there is little need to read between the lines.

Japanese communication is highly vague and intuitive, necessitating a great degree of reading between the lines. For example, communication takes place quite often without the use of complete sentences. Phrases are frequently sufficient to convey one's meaning. For example, the phrase "*sore wa*" (それは) by itself literally means "that is." It is certainly not a complete sentence and is useless in conveying any meaning in English. In Japanese, however, it is more than enough to communicate its meaning: "That is not what I had in mind." "That's not it." "That's off the mark." "That's wrong." "I disagree." Providing a properly nuanced translation requires being able to correctly interpret the context.

> Japanese communication is highly vague and intuitive, necessitating a great degree of reading between the lines.

This dynamic of communicating in incomplete sentences does not apply only to individual phrases used every so often in a conversation. Rather it applies to entire conversations as well, allowing for a majority of sentences in the conversation to be incomplete sentences. Specifically, the subject of a sentence is typically spoken once when the topic is first brought up. After that, it is not repeated. Incomplete sentences or phrases are commonly used after that. This is not such a problem when only one topic is being discussed; however, as a second, third, or even fourth topic is introduced into the conversation, each new subject will likewise not be repeated. As the conversation jumps from one topic to another without the subject of the sentence being stated, it becomes a real challenge to follow what is going on. It is "expected" that each participant will be able to follow the conversation intuitively.

> There is a whole realm of non-verbal communication that is highly developed and commonly used in Japanese society and business.

As a result of this highly intuitive nature of Japanese communication, there is a whole realm of non-verbal communication that is highly developed and commonly used in Japanese society and business. Needless to say, this presents another challenge to non-native speakers in learning the language. The three most common types of intuitive communication are:

- **Hara-gei** (腹芸): literally "belly talk" or subtle, stomach-to-stomach communication

- **Ishin-denshin** (以心伝心): "mind-to-mind transmission" or non-verbal, tacit understanding

- **Ammoku no ryoukai** (暗黙の了解): understanding through silence, which has the very Zen-like literal meaning of "the understanding of silence"

The highly intuitive nature of Japanese communication is also well expressed in the term commonly used to describe the essence of customer service in Japan: *omote nashi* (おもてなし).

While the literal dictionary meaning is simply "hospitality," its significance—like so much else in Asian communication and culture—is so much broader, deeper, and nuanced. It means to have the mindset to understand all things from the perspective of the client, to *intuitively* know what is needed, and make sure it is taken care of without the customer ever becoming aware of or asking for it.

In explaining how this great degree of vague, cryptic, and intuitive communication is possible, Japanese often point to the fact that they have been such a homogeneous society with one common culture and language for so long that everyone can somehow or other intuitively follow what is being communicated (*nanto naku wakaru* 何となく分かる).

In this regard, Japan's current Prime Minister, Abe Shinzo, aptly sums up the difficulty that foreign companies have communicating with Japanese counterparts when he wrote:

> *The Japanese have a reputation for being taciturn and hard to communicate with. Probably the most difficult part of Japanese communication for people from other countries is the way people here converse wordlessly.** — * **The Government of Japan, *We are Tomodachi (We are Friends)* (Tokyo: Office of the Prime Minister, Spring/Summer 2014), page 72.**

The wife of a close Japanese friend and former colleague once explained to me that this ability to intuitively understand each other in Japan is similar to the communication between a mother and her new born child. She noted that just as she could understand the unintelligible sounds of her new born children, adults in Japan can intuitively understand what is being said to each other. This intuitive communication in Japan would equate to the American experience expressed as "we just looked at each other and knew what the other was thinking."

V. MUTUAL CONNECTION AND INTERDEPENDENCE

In addition to having one shared culture, however, Japan's unique communication dynamics are possible because of what Japanese commonly characterize as feeling that all Japanese are organically connected to each other and to the greater whole. This concept comes in part from Japan's native Shinto religion that sees everyone as being connected and mutually dependent on each other, as well as from Taoism, the China-originated philosophy that teaches that we each are one small part of the greater interconnected universe.*

The sense of being mutually connected and interdependent, then, is a fundamental feature of Japanese society and is exhibited in the strong group orientation of the Japanese. This trait influences the Japanese approach to communication and business as well as the dynamics that define them. Both this connectivity and interdependence are well expressed in the following common expressions:

- **Okagesama de** (お陰様で)**:** This phrase translates into English as an equivalent to "thanks to everyone's

* For an in-depth examination of the impact of Shinto, Taoism, Confucianism, and Buddhism on Japan's business culture, see Robert Charles Azar. *Navigating Japan's Business Culture*. Raleigh, NC: Write Way Publishing Co., 2016.

assistance or cooperation."* This self-deprecating expression is typically used when one party is thanked for or is complimented by another party for a job well done. Rather than saying "You're welcome" or "Thank you," the party that completed the task responds with *okagesama de*—I was able to do it thanks to everyone's cooperation. Because everyone is mutually connected and dependent, it is possible for things to be accomplished because of the presence and role of everyone that is part of the greater whole. In other words, it is possible for things to get done not because of any one individual's action but because everyone in the group does their part and contributes to the overall scheme of things. What a contrast to the rugged individualism and self-sufficiency that informs American culture and communication.

This view that the role played by every individual is necessary for things to function is the reason why Japanese value and take seriously every job in a company from the chairman of the board all of the way down to the janitor. Everyone's role and contributions are important, necessary, and appreciated. This outlook, in turn, further reinforces the group-orientation idea that everyone is connected, interdependent, and part of the greater whole.

---

* Looking at the roots of *okagesama de*, it literally means "fortunately," "under the shadow of the gods" and "the way of the shade." This outlook stems from Japan's native Shinto religion as well as Taoism, and speaks to the notion that everyone is connected and all things are possible due to everyone. See *Navigating Japan's Business Culture* by Robert Charles Azar.

That everyone's role and contributions to the greater whole are to be valued is the reason why when asked what kind 'of work one does, Japanese always reply by stating only the name of the organization they work for, never the job function. For example, a Japanese would reply that he or she worked for Japan Airlines rather than identifying their specific position. In contrast, in the States, we reply by stating our job function—"I am an accountant." Because our culture is oriented around the individual and not the group, we often do not even give the name of our employer. For the Japanese, the employer name is all they say. Since all job functions are important and the culture is oriented around the group, it is the group one belongs to that is paramount in Japan. Hence, so much attention is focused on promoting smooth relationships and group harmony as noted throughout this book.

This notion of *okagesama de* is such a part of the Japanese mind-set and communication dynamic that often people have no idea who the "everyone" is when *okagesama de* is said to them. On countless occasions over the years, I have asked Japanese clients, associates, and friends whose help is being acknowledged when *okagesama de* was said to them. The answer was always a variation of "I don't know. But it is our way of respecting and being appreciative of everyone and all that went into allowing this to happen."

- **Osewa ni natte orimasu** (お世話になっておりま
  す): This means "I'm benefitting from your help"
  or "I'm able to do this thanks to your good graces."
  Japanese say this expression to each other even
  when in fact they have not been helped at all by
  anyone else. In using this phrase regularly, Japanese
  are confirming that everyone belongs to and is
  mutually dependent on the greater whole. So deeply
  embedded in Japan's culture and business practices
  is this idea that the phrase is commonly used as a
  greeting at the beginning of meetings, telephone
  conversations, emails, corporate newsletters, formal
  business correspondences, and official corporate
  announcements.

- **Yoroshiku onegai shimasu** (よろしくお願いします):
  This means "I'm counting on you." It also means
  "Thank you for your cooperation, understanding, or
  indulgence." The notion that Japanese are counting
  on others is again an affirmation of their mutual
  dependence and reliance on the group and greater
  whole.

  When Japanese are not sure they can satisfactorily
  do or provide something, they ask for the other
  party's understanding or indulgence by saying
  yoroshiku onegai shimasu—or "Thank you for
  understanding that what I provide may not be
  good enough." This self-deprecating expression is
  a way for Japanese to indulge (*amaeru* 甘える)
  the group by saying "Thank you for understanding
  if things do not proceed as well as I intend or

you may expect." In this way, the greater whole supports everyone and makes everything possible. Again, this is the cultural influence of Shinto and Taoism.

Japanese also commonly use *yoroshiku onegai shimasu* to express thanks and appreciation for each other's mutual cooperation and assistance. In that case, both parties use it, not just the receiving party.

The phrase is shortened to *yoroshiku* after which is added either the word *domo* (どうも which means "thanks") or *douzo* (どうぞ which means "please"). For example, if Mr. Tanaka is doing something for Mr. Suzuki, at the end of the conversation Mr. Suzuki will say *yoroshiku domo* which means "Thanks – I'm counting on your assistance." Mr. Tanaka will reply to that by saying *yoroshiku douzo*, which means "Please avail yourself of my help, I'm happy to oblige you." or "I'm likewise counting on your assistance—go ahead."

Upon visiting Japan, one of the first things foreigners notice is how often Japanese nod their heads to each other while talking. What truly baffles foreigners, however, is that Japanese will nod their heads to the other party even when talking on the telephone. Why would anyone nod their head to someone when the nod cannot be seen by the other party? The reason is that whether they can see you or not, everyone is still connected, so it is natural to offer head bows in recognition of and respect for that mutual connection whether it can be seen or not. Therefore, while it may seem odd to Westerners, it makes total sense within Japan's cultural context and communication dynamics to nod even if the other party cannot see it. This is another example of how, as we saw in chapter one, what is considered "rational thinking" in America and Asia can be quite dissimilar.

To counterbalance their sense that everyone is connected and mutually dependent and the weight that comes with that, Japanese have a unique way of differentiating between those with whom they are obligated to follow all of Japan's demanding cultural norms and expectations and those to whom they are not obligated. The people or parties that Japanese are obligated to are those who are on the "inside" of their group (*uchi* 内); those individuals or parties that Japanese are not obligated to are those on the "outside" (*soto* 外) of their group. Group means any entity an individual belongs to like their family, neighborhood, school, company, social club, team, or country.

What is noteworthy about this *uchi* versus *soto* differentiation is its impact on Japanese communication. Japanese do not have to relate and communicate in accordance with all the etiquette rules when dealing with those outside of their groups. For example, if the person is outside of their groups, they do not have to be concerned about who needs to bow more deeply. An equal bow suffices to outsiders. The nuances of bowing in Japanese culture and business are discussed later in this chapter.

The differentiation between insiders and outsiders also impacts information sharing. In America, we value free access to information and tend to be very open in sharing it. We even codify it in our laws, such as the Freedom of Information Act.

Japanese have a different attitude toward disclosing information which directly impacts negotiating in that market.

> Japanese have a different attitude toward disclosing information which directly impacts negotiating in that market.

In Japan, those on the inside are afforded more meaningful access to relevant information pertaining to business activities. Those on the outside less. Japanese will hold information very close to their vests and be very slow in divulging even information that is cursory in nature when they are in early dealings with foreign executives because the foreigners are still on the outside at that point.

As a trust relationship develops and a foreigner's status changes to that of an "insider," Japanese will be comfortable sharing more meaningful information with them. Accordingly, if Japanese are not as forthcoming as you would like with providing substantive information in your initial meetings, this is not necessarily a red flag. The amount of proprietary information they share with you will increase in proportion to the strength of the trust relationship you build with them. On the other hand, if they do not share more information over time, then it is clear they are not bringing you to the inside and, therefore, are not interested in engaging in business with you. As we can see, there is a direct correlation between the degree of information shared and the strength of the mutual relationship in Japan. In this way, information sharing is relational—that is, relationship contingent—in the Japanese market. Once again, we see the centrality and far-reaching influence of relationship.

VI. COMMUNICATING WITHOUT DIRECTLY DISAGREEING OR SAYING NO

We learned that it is deemed impolite to directly disagree, contradict, or say no to others, especially in formal settings or when the parties do not have a relationship, and we have learned that this cultural preference can be attributed to the importance and priority of group harmony in their culture. Japanese go to great lengths to avoid disrupting that harmony, including avoiding disagreeing or saying no at inappropriate times. This dynamic is shared throughout Asia.

We have also learned that Japanese society and language do have culturally accepted ways of expressing disagreement and saying no in appropriate circumstances and at appropriate times. There are three things in play when learning to disagree properly in Japan: the cultural preference for group harmony, the societal norms that govern politeness and showing respect, and the tendency, therefore, toward intentionally vague conversation unless the conversation is taking place in certain acceptable environments such as, for example, the after-meeting-meeting in the negotiating process between a third party intermediary and one of the companies (as discussed earlier) or an "evaluation meeting" (*hanseikai* (反省会).* So, let's look at ways Japanese communicate without creating undesired disharmony.

First, the Japanese language has quite an array of words or phrases that culturally convey "no" to the knowing hearer. It is noteworthy that nearly all the accepted words to use when disagreeing have a literal meaning that has nothing to do with saying

---

* *Hanseikai* is the meeting engaged in to evaluate business items for the purpose of openly discussing and identifying ways for continual improvement (*kaizen*). In Japan, this is done at the end of every work day, every week, month, quarter, and year. For detailed information on *hanseikai* meetings, see *Navigating Japan's Business Culture* by Robert Charles Azar.

"no." For example, even the word "yes" can mean "no." The following is a representative list of phrases used to offer a polite no. The list would not be complete without the word "no" itself.

1. Hai (はい): Yes
2. Chotto... (ちょっと...): A little
3. Sore wa... (それは...): That is...
4. Sore wa chotto... (それはちょっと...): That is a little...
5. Iya (イヤ): Not really
6. Dou deshou ne... (どうでしょうね...): Mmm, how about that?...
7. Saa... (さあ...): Well...
8. Jitsu wa... (実は...): Actually...
9. Honto wa... (本当は...): In truth...
10. Wakarimashita (分かりました): I understand.
11. Wakarimasen (分かりません): I do not know.
12. Kentou shimasu (検討します): That is worth our consideration.
13. Zensho shimasu (善処します): I will do my utmost best for that.
14. Suimasen (すいません): I am sorry.
15. Moushi wake nai (申し訳ない): I apologize.
16. Moshika shitara... (もしかしたら...): It could be such that...
17. Muzukashii desu... (難しいです): That's difficult.
18. Nanno koto deshou (何のことでしょう): What is that?
19. Ittai nanno koto deshou (一体何のことでしょう): What in the world...?
20. Sucking in air through your teeth
21. Replying with silence
22. Iie (いいえ): No.

To underscore the significance of understanding the power of an indirect no, the following is a true account of a state visit between the Japanese prime minister and the U.S. president where both the president, speaking in English, and the prime minister, speaking in Japanese, each reiterate their take on the Oval Office meeting they had just completed. The president expressed his pleasure at the fruitful outcome of the meeting, noting that the prime minister had agreed to the U.S.'s requests.

The prime minister echoed him on the fruitfulness of the meeting. Regarding the requests the president asked of Japan, the prime minister stated that he will *zensho shimasu* (善処します)—correctly translated literally into English as "I will do my utmost best for that." Both parties are pleased with that message. However, the two parties made contradictory statements regarding the outcome. While the literal meaning of the English statement is that America and Japan are in agreement regarding the requests, the actual cultural meaning of the Japanese phrase *zensho shimasu* is "I do not consent."

In this case, the American government now has certain expectations based on that meeting while the Japanese actually set very different expectations. That is because while the literal words say "I will do my utmost best for that," the actual cultural meaning is a definite no—a powerful example of a polite no in the relationship between the U.S. and one of its most important business partners and strategic allies.

When Japan does not attempt to implement any of the meeting items in the future, America concludes Japan was disingenuous. Japan, however, has a clean conscience because, according to their cultural norms, they not only clearly stated

> The actual cultural meaning of words and phrases sometimes has nothing to do with their literal meaning.

they could not agree but did so very politely.

As pointed out, foreigners almost always rely on Japanese to provide the translator when meeting. Because of Japan's code of respect, foreigners will only receive polite, literal translations. In order to understand the actual cultural meaning—what in fact is *actually* going on—foreigners must have a translator *on their team* who is in a position to provide accurate cultural interpretation. When they do not do this, the foreign company or executive is placed at a tactical and strategic disadvantage fraught with the possibilities of confusion, misunderstanding, and false expectations. The need for such a facilitator interpreter is analyzed in the next chapter.

Now that awareness has been raised about the ways used by Japanese to disagree, the question becomes how can you, speaking in English, express your disagreement without offending your potential business partner? As noted in section II of chapter three, I have found two methods that work very well to allow polite disagreement with your Asian partner.

The response "That might be difficult" translates well into Japanese—*Sore wa muzukashii kamo shiremasen* (それは難しいかもしれません). You are not directly saying no, but you are indicating you are not in a position to agree. I like the Zen touch this response offers that leaves open the possibility of a different answer in the future.

An effective second way to handle disagreement is to reply

with a counterproposal. Verbally recognize their approach as one option, and then ask if XYZ would be another option. This allows you to come across as being open-minded and considerate of your partner's interests. A benefit to this approach is being able to offer a more desirable option for you that still could serve the interests of both parties.

The wording used in this option is very important. When Americans offer a counterproposal, we typically phrase it: "*I have an alternative option.*" By saying "*I have,*" the alternative becomes the idea of the person saying it—the American executive. Using the words "*would another option be*" instead of "*I have* an alternative" leaves the ownership of the idea up for grabs. Allowing the Japanese to take your suggestion as a variation or substitute for their own makes it easier for them to accept it and later lobby for that idea within their company, and it demonstrates you are a partner concerned about the interests of both companies.

In the case of the Japanese language, the counterproposal would have automatically been offered as "would another option be" since, as discussed earlier in this chapter, "I" as the subject of the sentence would have naturally been omitted. This is another example of how the purpose of communication in Japan and the dynamics underpinning it focus on promoting the mutual interest of and smooth relations between all parties involved. As noted throughout this book, it is precisely these types of differences that result in dissimilar approaches, dynamics, and protocols in negotiating in Japan and other Asian markets.

The communication dynamic that it is not polite to say "no" directly or disagree is prevalent throughout much of Asia. In China, for instance, it is customary to use alternative actions and phrases as the Japanese do for expressing disagreement and saying "no." Examples would include:

- Become silent

- Change the subject to another matter

- Reply with a question on the same or different topic

- Use phrases such as:
  o *Hai xing/ hai ke yi* – appears fairly passable
  o *Hai bu cuo* – seems not wrong
  o *Hai hao* – seems fairly all right

While this same dynamic is common in Korea, negotiators in Korea interrupt and directly say "no" to a much greater degree than in China or Japan. In addition, they often say "no" more forcefully than their counterparts in the rest of the Far East and the rest of Asia, just as they haggle and bargain in a much more animated fashion as noted in chapter two.

VII. LITERAL VS. CULTURAL MEANING

When I was working in a Japanese company early on in my involvement with Japan before I became a speaker of Japanese, I had an interesting experience that highlights another very prominent feature of the Japanese language.

The president of the company I was working for at that time and I were waiting for the elevator. When the elevator door opened, an employee said to the president *"ohayou gozaimasu"*

(おはようございます) as she got off the elevator. This means "good morning." The president replied, *"doumo"* (どうも) which, according to the dictionary, means "thanks." I thought to myself that was rather an arrogant response—the employee says "good morning" and the president replies "thanks." As the company president and I were close friends, I felt comfortable asking him about that exchange. He laughed and said that while *doumo* literally does mean "thanks," it also is culturally understood to mean "the same to you."

The problem is that "thanks" is given as the meaning of *doumo* in the dictionary, but "the same to you" is not. As this example illustrates, an additional challenge inherent in Japanese communication is that words and phrases often have cultural meanings not listed in the dictionary in addition to their literal definitions.

The actual cultural meaning of words and phrases sometimes has nothing to do with their literal meaning. Here are some common examples.

- **Doumo** (どうも)**:** The literal meaning of *doumo* is "thanks," while also having a cultural meaning of "the same to you."

- **Sore wa** (それは)**:** The literal, dictionary meaning of this phrase is "that is." However, it is also used to expresses disagreement, disapproval, or dissatisfaction. For example: "That is not agreeable." "That is mistaken." "That is not what I had said." Or it can simply mean "no."

- **Chotto** (ちょっと)**:** Despite its literal meaning

of "a little,"*chotto* also is used to express a negative response to what is being discussed.

- **Iie** (いいえ): This is the word for "no." In Japanese, however, "no" does not necessarily only mean no— it can be part of the polite process for saying "yes"!

  By way of explanation, if someone is offering something significant, it is not polite to immediately accept the offer. The more significant the item is, the more immodest it would be to accept it right away. Instead, it is polite to go through the protocol of saying "no, thank you" three times and then after saying "no" to the third offer, to say "yes," thereby in the end accepting what is offered.

  This interchange is similar to an American initially replying "no, thank you" to something being offered and then subsequently replying "yes" by saying something like "well, since you twisted my arm."

  As Japanese are very self-deprecating, it is considered presumptuous and immodest to reply "yes" to receiving something important before saying no three times.

An additional challenge for foreigners in communicating in Japan is that this discrepancy between the literal definition and the actual cultural meaning applies not only to words but also to business actions and concepts. One example is when managers in Japanese companies are given desks by themselves in front of windows. In America, getting a window desk is seen as a positive development, a reward, or perhaps part of a promotion. In Japan, however, the meaning of that same action is quite different. Known as "a person by the window" (*mado giwa zoku* 窓ぎわ族), the person is being told by the company that his future lies outside the window—that is, outside the company.

> This discrepancy between the literal and the actual cultural meaning applies also to business actions and concepts.

Another differing cultural meaning of a business action is that of an offer of an honorary position in a company or organization. In the States, we offer an honorary position to solidify the good working relationship between two parties or in recognition of assistance provided. In Japan, offering an honorary position is a polite way of asking someone to become one of the major financial investors in the entity.

Thus, not only the Japanese language but also business customs, concepts, and actions are full of instances where the cultural meaning—the actual meaning in the conduct of business—is different from, even completely unrelated to, the literal meaning of what is said or done. Given that the discrepancy in meaning lies with the cultural, not literal meaning, this problem is persistent even when Asian executives negotiate speaking in English. This dynamic is a serious obstacle that often negatively impacts Western executives in their negotiations and conduct of business with Asian firms. In addition, it underscores the need for U.S. companies to have their own in-house facilitator interpreter, as explored in chapter five.

From these examples, it is clear there can be two levels of reality in Japanese communication. There is what appears to be the case literally as well as what actually is the reality of the situation. So prevalent and socially sanctioned is this facet of Japanese culture, communication, and business that the Japanese have distinct words to clearly identify and express these two meanings and realities.

> "Tatemae" is what is ostensibly the case. "Honne" means the actual situation.

The first word is *tatemae* (建前). The meaning of these two *kanji* characters is "constructed façade" and means what is ostensibly the case or meaning. It represents what is apparently the situation, or seemingly the meaning, or supposedly the case.

The second word is *honne* (本音). These two *kanji* characters mean "the actual sound." *Honne* means the actual situation or meaning. It is what is actually going on, what rings true, the reality.

Both the Japanese language and culture go to great lengths to differentiate between what the apparent situation and meaning are and what the actual situation and meaning are as a way to show proper respect, follow proper protocol, and maintain and promote group harmony.

It would disrupt harmony within the company and be disrespectful to directly and abruptly say to a manager who has dedicated many years working for the company that he is no longer needed and to find employment elsewhere. That would be the *honne,* the actual situation. Instead, to avoid upsetting the smooth relationships within the company and to avoid anyone losing face, senior management expresses the same point to him by taking the indirect *tatemae* action of giving him a window desk by itself. The earlier example of the miscommunication between the U.S. president and the Japanese prime minister is another example of *tatemae* and *honne*.

While highly prevalent in Japan and many markets throughout Asia, we have little tolerance for this type of communication in America. The *tatemae* and *honne* dynamic would be considered duplicitous and sour other people's desire to interact with you. Meanwhile, the opposite is true in Japan. I believe the reader can easily imagine how having to deal with the two realities of *tatemae* and *honne* can be highly problematic for American executives both in negotiating and subsequently working together with companies in Japan, China, Korea, and other Asian markets, especially if the foreign executives are not even aware this socially acceptable dynamic exists.

VIII. SILENCE IN COMMUNICATION

Silence during communication is not viewed favorably in the U.S. We are not comfortable with it. It feels awkward, and we rush to fill it. When we experience silence in negotiations or conversations, we are concerned that it means the other party has lost interest or may be upset. In fact, when we get angry with someone and deliberately stop talking to them, we call it "giving them the silent treatment." In Japan's culture, however, silence is perceived quite differently.

In Japan, silence can be used in communication to sharpen one's attention to the discussion at hand or as a pause in the discussion to be used to sift through and digest what is being discussed. Japanese will even close their eyes during silence to fully focus on using silence as an opportunity to listen carefully to or reflect on the points being made. In addition, silence is the only time that Japan's non-verbal communication methods discussed earlier—such as *ammoku no ryokai* (暗黙の了解) or understanding through silence—can take place. In these ways, silence is a common part of communication in Japan. It cannot always be viewed negatively and certainly not as something that must be filled.

Silence can also mean disagreement. Accordingly, when negotiating, how can one discern whether Japanese executives are using silence to digest what is being said or if they are disagreeing? Japanese reply to that question by saying they just know—they can sense it. This would be a practical example of the types of intuitive communication discussed in section IV of this chapter.

For non-Japanese, discerning the answer lies in what Japanese executives say after they break their silence. If their initial comment immediately after the silence is favorable about what was being discussed, then it is clear they were simply focusing on it. If what they say is not positive—that is, negative or even just neutral—that is an indication of either lack of interest or lack of agreement. Likewise, if they break the silence by ignoring what you last stated or change the subject, that also indicates they are not in agreement.

Knowing that Westerners are not comfortable with silence, Japanese do occasionally use it as a negotiating tool in business discussions to frustrate foreign parties and trip them up. When

Japanese executives engage in silence, Americans worry that they have lost interest or are upset, that the negotiations might fall apart. U.S. executives rush to fill the silence by softening their previously stated position, thinking this is necessary to salvage the interest of the Japanese firm and keep the negotiation on track. Recognizing this, Japanese companies may use silence as a negotiating tool to win more favorable conditions. While only occasionally utilized in Japan, this negotiating dynamic is prevalent in China, Korea, and other Asian markets.

How long can this silence last? Anywhere from a few seconds to a few minutes. It can be a truly daunting situation as the entire room goes silent and the Japanese stare down at the table. The longest period of silence I have experienced in negotiations in Japan was about two-and-a-half minutes.

What is the best way for foreigners to deal with silence when communicating with Asians? Do not rush to fill it or ask if anything is wrong. Instead, respect and maintain the silence. Quietly sit and wait it out, perhaps by reviewing the points you have just made or will address next. Alternatively, enjoy a Zen moment of reprieve and reflection. Even better, closing your eyes during the silence totally turns upside down their attempts to use silence as a negotiating tactic. This is an example of when you know the communication dynamics at play in negotiating, you can not only avoid those challenges but actually leverage them to advance the interests of your firm.

The key to dealing with silence in negotiating is to demonstrate that you are not in the least fazed by the silence. Allow the Japanese to break the silence. When they are ready—that is, when they have had sufficient time to reflect on what has just been discussed or when they realize that using silence as a negotiating tool will not work with you—they will resume the discussion.

During the silence, it would be viewed as unprofessional and disrespectful to your Japanese counterparts to engage in an activity not related to the discussion at hand. For example, do not check for messages on your phone, boot up your computer, take out a newspaper, adjust your watch to local time, get coffee, leave the meeting to use the restroom, communicate with your company colleagues by writing notes or other non-verbal means, or walk around the room.

There is another interesting aspect to silence in negotiating. During these silences, Japanese break off all eye contact. Given the importance of constantly maintaining good eye contact when communicating in our culture, this deliberate and long break in eye contact by Japanese is another reason why the Japanese use of silence causes American executives to feel so uncomfortable. In our culture, deliberately breaking and avoiding eye contact is a way to communicate dissatisfaction or the outright end of communication. It is common for American executives to mis-interpret not only the lack of dialogue but also the lack of eye contact during silence from Japanese.

What is the best way to navigate this Japanese negotiating tactic? In addition to respecting the silence, hold your ground after it concludes—that is, do not soften your negotiating position. If they engaged in silence to express strong disagreement with your last point, when they end the silence, they will offer a counterproposal or move on to another topic. If they were favorably contemplat-ing what you were saying, they will reply accordingly. Conditions either way are then right to continue the negotiation dialogue.

IX. RESPECT AND COMMUNICATION DYNAMICS

Japanese society is well known for the priority it places on showing great respect to one another and following established protocol. This is true in China, Korea, and most other Asian nations as well. There are numerous ways that respect is demonstrated. Two major ways it is demonstrated in communication are the bow and the use of polite language. Let's explore these dynamics unique to communication in Asian countries.

The bow is ubiquitous in Japan. It is an integral part of interaction in all areas and all levels of Japanese society, including business. However, in Japan a bow is not simply just a bow. Like so many things there, the bow is its own ritualized art form that possesses great significance. The bow is used to demonstrate different levels of respect, and it does so in two fundamental ways.

> The bow is its own ritualized art form that possesses great significance.

The initial way is the level to which the parties bow to each other. There are three levels of bows. The first is the head nod in which the person slightly nods the head forward fifteen degrees. The upper torso remains straight and just the head moves forward slightly. This demonstrates the lowest degree of respect. This head bow is used by those of greater status to those of lesser status.

The second bow is the middle bow. This is when the upper body comes down thirty degrees. This represents the middle range of respect and is used between parties of comparable hierarchical status.

The third bow is the full bow in which the upper torso comes down a full forty-five degrees. This is used by those having lower status to those in higher positions and expresses the greatest degree of respect.

If a company president is meeting individuals of lower status, he would only use the head bow while the others of lower ranking would engage in the full bow, lowering their upper bodies a full forty-five degrees.

Secondly, the bow expresses different levels of respect not only by how deep it is but also by how long it is held. The deeper the bow, the longer the individual must hold it. While the company president just nods his head down and up in one quick motion, a middle bow between individuals of comparable status is held one or two seconds, and subordinates will hold their full bow in the forty-five-degree position for a full three seconds.

> The bow expresses different levels of respect not only by how deep it is but also by how long it is held.

An additional manner in which different levels of respect are expressed in Japan is through various levels of politeness in the language used in communicating with others. Both written and spoken Japanese are structured such that several different levels of respect can be demonstrated through them. Specifically, this is done through verb conjugation and multiple versions of phrases, each with the same meaning but differing levels of politeness.

Verbs typically can be conjugated in multiple ways. Each different conjugation expresses a greater level of respect, going from a greater degree of closeness or familiarity in the relationship to a greater degree of respect and formality. For example, here are twelve different ways in which the verb "to drink" can be conjugated when asking if someone would like something to drink.

1. Nomu? 飲む?
2. Nomu-ka? 飲むか?
3. Nomanai? 飲まない?
4. Nomanai-ka? 飲まないか?
5. Nomimasu? 飲みます?
6. Nomimasu-ka? 飲みますか?
7. Nomimasen? 飲みません?
8. Nomimasen-ka? 飲みませんか?
9. Nomaremasu -ka? 飲まれますか?
10. Nomaremasen-ka? 飲まれませんか?
11. O-nomuni narimasu-ka? お飲みになりますか?
12. O-nomini narimasen-ka? お飲みになりませんか?

All twelve of the above words are identical in meaning—"Would you like something to drink?" However, they vary in the degree of respect they express. The longer the phrase, the higher the number on the list above, the more respect the verb demonstrates.

As this example illustrates, the options for showing different levels of respect through verb conjugation are quite numerous. However, having so many options is cumbersome and therefore not always practical for trying to figure out which of these many forms of conjugation parties should use in addressing each other. In business, Japanese typically use three levels of politeness in both spoken and written Japanese to express the proper level of respect to each other. Those three levels are:

- **Sonkei-go** 尊敬語: the *respectful form* which elevates the other party and is the most respectful

- **Teinei-go** 丁寧語: the *polite form* which is used between parties of comparable status (です, ます)

- **Kenjo-go** 謙譲語: the *humble form* which lowers oneself (いただく)

By way of example, here are the three different ways of saying "to drink" in these three levels of politeness:

- **Onomini narimasu** お飲みになります: the respectful form

- **Nomimasu** 飲みます: the polite form

- **Itadakimasu** いただきます: the humble form

As we can see, the etiquette protocols and communication dynamics in Japanese society are very involved, and they can be complex and cumbersome. These protocols and dynamics add another layer of difficulty to the challenges foreigners face conducting business in Japanese. It is important that foreign executives recognize how important formality, proper form, and showing respect are in the Japanese market and throughout Asia. American companies should make it standard policy to require any employees going abroad to engage in business to undergo proper intercultural training in these areas.

X. SIGNIFICANCE OF THE BUSINESS CARD RITUAL

Japanese are very deliberate when exchanging business cards. They present and receive business cards with both hands and take a moment to study the business card while the person is still standing in front of them. It is only after that moment of silently examining the card that they continue their interaction with that person.

Westerners have suggested that the reason is so the individuals can identify which *kanji* characters are used in writing the other party's name. The comparable situation in America would be to examine a business card to confirm whether Mr. Smith spelled his name "Smith" or "Smyth." While there may on occasion be a need to confirm what *kanji* are used in writing the person's name, there are other reasons that are much more fundamental and significant behind this action.

First, the exchange of business cards signifies that a connection (*kone* コネ) has been established. That has tremendous import in Japan. With that, it is now both possible and proper to begin communication with each other. Without having a connection, it is not socially accepted to initiate contact with another party. So inextricably linked are having a connection and communication that in the Japanese language the word for "communication" also means "connection" (*renraku* 連絡).

Because of this communication dynamic, cold calling does not work in Japan. One either needs to be introduced to the other party or to have the occasion to exchange business cards and establish a connection and thereby be able to commence communication with them.

Besides making it possible to contact another party, exchanging business cards socially obligates the other party to respond. In short, exchanging business cards is a prerequisite for initiating communication and a new business relationship. Given this importance, having the opportunity to exchange business cards as well as doing so properly in accordance with cultural protocol is of great significance. That is why Japanese exchange business cards with the seriousness of purpose and deliberateness with which they do.

> Because of this communication dynamic, cold calling does not work in Japan.

Given the power—and inherent obligation—of the business card exchange, it is quite common for company chairmen, presidents, and other VIP's in Japan to deliberately not carry their business cards with them. By not carrying their business cards with them, they can avoid the business card exchange. They can thereby remain free from the obligation to have to respond when they have no interest in communicating with a party who approaches them because, without exchanging business cards, no connection was established.

Simply receiving a card does not constitute a business card exchange. Each party must give his or her card and receive the other party's card in order for an exchange to occur. Only then are both parties in a position to communicate. As those high-level executives do not want to be without their business cards in the event they meet someone with whom they would like to connect, they have their assistants carry their business cards. They are readily available for exchange—but only at the discretion of these high-ranking executives. When they are interested in exchanging business cards, they will instruct their subordinate to present their card to the subordinate of the other party.

The second reason business cards carry such great significance in Japan is that they are a primary means for determining what level of respect parties need to demonstrate to each other. As we have seen, Japanese society is strictly hierarchical and both business and social etiquette dictate that the parties show proper levels of respect to each other according to their respective status. The business card is the only way an individual can know what their standing is relative to the person they are meeting, and based on that, what level of politeness is required. That is why Japanese intently study the card the instant they receive it—to determine their relative status to each other.

> The reason business cards carry such great significance is that they are a primary means for determining what level of respect parties need to demonstrate to each other.

The person in the lower hierarchical position needs to relate to individuals with a higher standing with a greater degree of respect. Conversely, the person with the higher standing need not express as great a degree of politeness to individuals with lower standing. As discussed above, those different degrees of politeness are expressed through the bow and the level of politeness in language used. The only way individuals meeting for the first time can know their relative status with each other is this ritual of the business card exchange.

Given the significance and important role that business

cards have, they are treated with great respect in Japan. They are always presented and received with both hands—never just one hand. Never, ever slide a card across the table to the other party. And also, unlike in America, it is not appropriate to write on a business card.

Japanese always keep business cards in a high-quality business card carrying case—generally made out of leather. After business cards are exchanged in a meeting and the parties sit down at the table, they do not stack those cards or immediately place them in their pocket or business card case. Instead, once seated, Japanese will line up the business cards they received in front of them on the table corresponding to where those individuals are seated across the table.

In a final step of demonstrating respect, Japanese will elevate the business card they received from the senior most person in the other party by placing it on top of their business card case on the table. As the senior most executive is usually sitting at the middle of the table as discussed in chapter three, his elevated card will be in the center of the row of business cards for those sitting on the other side of the table. In this way, greater respect is shown for the senior most executive of the other company.

In Japan, business cards are viewed as a symbol of one's company, just as a flag is a symbol of one's country. This symbolism is another reason business cards are treated with great respect and why writing on a Japanese business card is considered inappropriate and unprofessional.

When engaging in business with Japanese, Americans should always prepare bilingual English-Japanese business cards to allow the Japanese not only to keep track of your name and that of your company but also, as described above, to better understand what your standing is in your company. Japanese are more comfortable interacting with foreigners who are on a similar level in their respective company, so receiving a bilingual business card will assist them in figuring out that status.

Along with preparing bilingual business cards, it is always beneficial to send to the Japanese who will be in the negotiating meetings the profiles of all those on your team who will be joining the discussion, including their department name and their title. It is wise to include a professional headshot for each profile as well.

The importance of the business card is shared in China and Korea, though not engaged in with the same degree of exactness as in Japan.

It is advisable that U.S. companies prepare bilingual business cards for each market where they seek to engage in business. While doing so involves a minimal expense, preparing bilingual cards goes a long way in helping your negotiation meetings get off to a smooth start. More importantly, they clearly state to the Asian firms you meet with that their market has priority importance to you and your company.

XI. COMMUNICATION PROTOCOL

We have already noted it is not polite to directly disagree, contradict, or say no to others in formal meetings. As is true with so much in Japanese culture, there is a proper time and place to negotiate and engage in substantive communication.

Negotiations and formal business discussions can often be more ceremonial than substantive in Japan. They are often the opportunity to confirm formally what has been informally discussed and decided outside of the official meetings. Once negotiations have commenced, a common practice is for key participants from both parties to meet in smaller, unofficial meetings to discuss the substantive points. These discussions will be more open and candid than in the formal negotiating sessions. These meetings are one of the appropriate times and places to freely express contrary opinions and work to resolve points of disagreement directly.

This dynamic of the discussions in negotiations being ceremonial and discreet is more common in the initial stages of the relationship between the parties. As a trust relationship is established, communication in official meetings may become more open and candid.

Another common way to express contrary opinions in Japan is through third parties such as intermediaries who may have introduced the two parties, mutual business partners, banks, consultants, or attorneys. Because these intermediaries are third parties and not the principals, they are not bound by the same rules of etiquette the principal parties are and, therefore, can candidly relay and work to resolve conflicting opinions, sparing the main parties from having to do so. This is done to avoid potential friction and promote smooth relationships.

When conflicts do arise in Japan, it is expected that the principal parties will meet face-to-face and work out their differences in good faith. If they are not able to do this, they will utilize the assistance of a third party or parties. In the end, if the principals still are not able to resolve their conflict, it reflects negatively on *both* parties—both the aggrieved party as well as the party responsible for causing the problem. The result is that both parties lose face in the eyes of society, which is never desirable in the Japanese business community or in society at large.

> Just as there is an appropriate time to discuss substantive business matters, there are appropriate places as well.

Just as there is an *appropriate time* to discuss substantive business matters in Japan, there are *appropriate places* to do so as well. As a reminder from chapter three, customary venues for discussing substantive business matters include the following:

- Formal business meetings held in official business venues such as either company's office or factory, the offices of an intermediary if involved, a meeting room in a hotel or conference center, etc.

- During meals – particularly if the Asian executives initiate

- Over evening drinks

- On the golf course

Representative examples of places where substantive business topics are not discussed include:

- In the lobby of a hotel or company offices

- In hallways

- In elevators

- On the street

- In taxis or other cars

- In rest rooms

- While walking

Other communication dynamics and protocol items to avoid when communicating with Japanese and other Asian executives include the following:

- **Humor:** What is humorous in one culture might not be so in another. While it is common in America to start a presentation or meeting with a joke to break the ice and help everyone relax and feel comfortable, this custom does not exist in Japan. In Japan, humor has no place in negotiations or other formal business discussions. In addition, it is very difficult for humor to be understood and translated appropriately from one culture to another, and, accordingly, American executives should avoid using humor when negotiating in most international markets.

- **Slang:** This is difficult to be understood and translated correctly.

- **Double negatives:** They are confusing and difficult to translate. For instance, "We wouldn't disagree with your strategy." or "I can't not agree with your proposal." If the translator is skilled enough to be able to figure out the meaning of such double negative sentences, the amount of time needed to figure it out is time not following the subsequent conversation. The result is that you will lose translation of that part of what is being said. Either way, the use of double negatives impedes complete and accurate interpretation of business discussions.

- **Idioms:** For the most part, idioms are misunderstood and, therefore, translated incorrectly. As a result, they can cause significant confusion in business discussions. As you can imagine, the following idiom examples translated literally into any Asian language would be perplexing:
  - o "We had to cancel our outdoor marketing event because it was raining cats and dogs."
  - o "My company's CEO was so upset with my counterproposal that I was thrown under the bus."
  - o "There is more than one way to skin that cat."

To share a specific example, I have witnessed the "I was thrown under the bus" idiom being used on multiple occasions. In one instance, it was translated literally by the Japanese company's translator, and all of the Japanese were quite shocked to hear that the American executive had been thrown under a bus.

During a subsequent coffee break, two senior Japanese executives pulled me aside to ask me about the international sales director having been "thrown under the bus." One asked if the American CEO was truly that much of a madman, that crazy. He said he was not sure his company would want to do business with that company. The second executive said, "On the other hand, if their sales director survived being run over by a bus, perhaps we *should* work with their company. Who knows what other miracles he might be able to perform."

- **Sarcasm:** This is highly difficult for interpreters to understand. The result is that it is usually mistranslated, causing confusion.

- **Long and compound sentences:** The longer the sentence you use, the more difficult it is for the translator to keep up and appropriately translate it. There is a direct inverse correlation between length of the sentence and the accuracy and completeness of the translation: the longer the sentence, the more unlikely it is to be translated both fully and accurately.

> There is a direct inverse correlation between length of the sentence and the accuracy and completeness of translation.

I mention both fully and accurately. Longer, more complex sentences often result in the translator translating part of the sentence, but not translating the complete English thought in an effort to keep up with the ongoing conversation. This results in incomplete communication. If you cannot be confident the whole of the English was translated, you cannot be sure the Japanese have received your entire message. Likewise, if the Japanese say they agree with your position, you cannot be certain they are referring to or agreeing with all of your position points or just those that happened to be translated—and translated correctly.

- **Speaking in long intervals:** Just as using long sentences increases the likelihood of weak and inaccurate translation, speaking in long stretches likewise is a constant obstacle to complete and accurate interpretations.

> The longer the speaking interval, the greater the likelihood of incomplete and inaccurate translation.

For example, speaking for two or three minutes and then pausing for translation is a much higher hurdle for the translator than stopping after twenty or thirty seconds to allow for translation. When making very important points, it is better to break up key sentences into parts to allow for full and accurate translation, part by part, than to risk an incomplete or inferior translation. The longer the speaking interval, the greater the likelihood of incomplete and inaccurate translation. Speaking in smaller snippets will increase the effectiveness of your communication and promote a more effective negotiation.

When confronted with a long statement by an American executive, translators who work for the Asian company you are negotiating with may ask you to repeat parts of it in an attempt to translate your entire thought. However, translators who are hired from outside translation services often do not. This is so for two reasons.

First, unlike employees of the Asian firm, the hired translator has no vested interest in the outcome of the discussion. Secondly, they fear that having to ask the foreign executive to repeat what he/she said will result in the Asian firm that hired them giving them a low or negative evaluation when the translation service asks the Asian company for its feedback. This problem is quite common throughout Asia. It speaks to the inadvisability of utilizing outside translation services when negotiating. The best solution I have found for this is discussed at length in the next chapter.

- **Body language and hand gestures:** In Western countries, body language and hand gestures can play a significant part in communication. A frown, shaking your head, or rolling your eyes powerfully express that you are not interested or not in agreement. Hand gestures can be used to give added emphasis to a statement—such as pointing your index finger as you state your point. A thumbs-up or OK hand gesture can replace saying an entire sentence. These forms of communication are common in America. In Japan and throughout most of Asia, however, body language and hand gestures are not used when communicating.

- **Physical contact:** Japanese traditionally do not use physical contact when communicating. While younger or more internationally experienced Japanese will readily shake hands when meeting foreigners, unlike Westerners, Japanese do not hug or kiss when greeting each other. Japanese are usually greatly embarrassed by these gestures. Instead, they are accustomed to bowing to the other party when saying hello and goodbye.

  When Americans feel a connection with the other party, we may reach out and touch their forearm or hand while making a point or slap the other party on the back to express camaraderie or pleasure with a favorable conversation. This type of physical contact is not done in Japan and most of Asia and should be avoided.

- **Eye Contact:** It is important to note that Japanese do not engage in eye contact to the degree that Westerners do. While in our culture it is rude *not* to maintain good eye contact when speaking with someone, the opposite is true in Japan. It is impolite to maintain continuous, direct eye contact. Instead Japanese will typically glance at your eyes for two or three seconds and then rotate their glance to look at a few other places on your person, before returning for a quick glance at your eyes again.

> It is impolite
> to maintain
> continuous, direct
> eye contact.

For instance, after a quick glance at your eyes, their eyes will fix on one of your shoulders for a bit, then your necktie, then the other shoulder. They will then return for a quick two or three second glance at your eyes and repeat the process again. Younger or more internationally experienced Japanese typically maintain more direct eye contact in their discussions with foreigners.

It is a result of all of these different dynamics simultaneously at play that the level of translation accuracy in negotiations is surprisingly low. As noted at the beginning of this chapter, the average level of accurate and complete understanding between American and Asian companies engaging in negotiations ranges between seventy and ninety percent in my experience. The most effective solution for this problem is for American executives to prepare their own in-house facilitator interpreter.

INSIGHTS

We have seen in this chapter that the way Japanese approach communication is remarkably different from the approach commonly found in America, and this has a profound impact on both the progress and outcome of negotiations. Here is a list of a dozen representative differences:

- Having different goals for communication

- Using highly intuitive means of communication

- Using communication to reinforce a sense of mutual connection and interdependence

- Following complex cultural rules for saying no or disagreeing

- Using the cultural meaning of words, concepts, and actions that often have nothing to do with the literal meaning of those words, concepts, or actions

- Socially condoning the use of both *tatemae* (what is ostensibly the case) and *honne* (what is actually the case) in communication to promote smooth relationships and group harmony

- Using different communication dynamics for those parties who are on the inside (*uchi*) and those who are on the outside (*soto*)

- Using silence both as thinking time to reflect and further focus on the discussion and as a tactical tool in negotiating with foreigners

- Having different sensibilities regarding physical contact and maintaining continuous eye contact

- Having appropriate times and venues for substantive business discussions

- Having different protocols for demonstrating the proper level of respect

- Attaching greater significance to business cards, including the ritual of their exchange

As a result of the significant differences from Western communication, communicating in Japan can be like working through a maze. This is true not only for foreigners, but even for native Japanese themselves.

Westerners going to Asia often are concerned about being polite enough and not insulting their local hosts there, especially potential business partners. While this is certainly important, this chapter illustrates

Communicating in Japan can be like working through a maze—even for native Japanese themselves.

that the real challenges arising from different communication dynamics are much more fundamental and far reaching. They are ever-present in negotiations and function as powerful determinants of a negotiation's outcome.

Not knowing these different communication dynamics and how to effectively navigate them will directly reduce the level of success U.S. companies attain in each and every negotiating session and in business in general in Asia—from simply limiting a company's success to hindering the obtaining of optimal levels of success. We will look at options American executives can utilize in negotiating to successfully recognize, deal with, and leverage for their own advantage these challenges in chapter five.

CHAPTER 5

CRITICAL ROLE OF THE FACILITATOR INTERPRETER:
Interpreting Beyond Language and Beyond Language Interpreting

Translation is not a matter of words only: it is a matter of making intelligible a whole culture. — **Anthony Burgess**

The translator's role in international business is monumentally significant. Nowhere is this truer than in negotiating between countries and cultures. Despite that, however, it is typically overlooked. It should be a priority for any company that wants to maximize success and minimize risk in any geographical area. This chapter will explain the intricacies and importance of the critical role of the interpreter in international negotiation. It will also demonstrate how relying on a traditional translator is detrimental to a company's interests. This book is unique in claiming that executives need a facilitator interpreter, not a traditional translator.

Despite its importance, it is common practice on the part of American companies to give little, if any, consideration to the translator's role or significance. I cannot count the times that preparing a translator for meetings with foreign companies was not even discussed by or placed on the U.S. company's preparation check list. American companies pay a tremendous price in terms of time, effort, expense, and results and put themselves at a strategic and tactical disadvantage vis-à-vis Asian companies even before they depart their home offices for Asia if they do not have an appropriate interpreter on their team.

American companies take for granted that someone in the Asian company they meet with will speak English. After all, English has been the international language of business since it replaced French after World War II. Or if no one in the Asian company speaks English, then the thinking goes that surely the company will arrange for a translator with the assumption that it is the responsibility of those who need help conducting business in English to arrange for a translator for themselves. Such is the common attitude regarding the translator.

It is important to realize that the potential role and contribution of the translator goes well beyond translating the words of negotiation dialogue. As this chapter explains, the role of the translator should be central in a U.S. company's efforts to suc-ceed abroad. There are several fundamental reasons for this. Let's explore them.

I. LOST IN CULTURAL TRANSLATION: THE NEED FOR CULTURAL FLUENCY AND INTERPRETATION

A.   IMPACT OF CULTURE

Western executives commonly believe that the desired trans-lator for international negotiating is one who is fluent in the two languages involved. However, this is only half correct. To be fully effective, a translator must not only be fluent in both English and the language of the Asian company but also equally fluent and comfortable with the cultures of both countries. No matter how fluent translators may be in the languages, they will never be able to convey fully and accurately what both sides are attempting to communicate if they do not also understand the cultures of each country.

We have seen in previous chapters many ways cultural understanding, or the lack of it, can impact negotiations and doing business in Asia in general. Without the cultural understanding, a translator at best can only provide literal translations of what is being said. While literal translations may be correct "word for word" renditions, such translations often do not convey the whole meaning of the message,

> Literal translations often fail to capture the *actual meaning* of what is being said.

as discussed in chapter four. Worse yet, these literal translations may not deliver the intended message given the communication dynamics of Asian languages and cultures. Literal translations often fail to capture the cultural connotations, nuances, implied meanings, and built-in but unspoken expectations—that is, *the actual meaning*—of what is being said. A translator can only convey the cultural connotations and nuances of the speaker if the translator knows the connotations and nuances of both cultures equally well and, equally important, understands the necessity of incorporating them into the translations.

Let's look at some examples in the Japanese language. The phrase *kentou shimasu* (検討します) is a common response in that language. It is used by the party that is listening to an idea or proposal (for instance, a Japanese company) in responding to the party that is presenting that idea or proposal (for instance, an American firm). This phrase is invariably translated into English as: "That is worth our consideration." In an American cultural context, these words are taken as a somewhat positive response.

While that is the correct literal translation of that phrase, what does not get translated into English is the actual Japanese cultural meaning, which is "We are not at all interested." So, while that phrase is taken as a favorable response by the foreign company, in reality, the Japanese party is conveying the exact opposite message. When the translator provides the literal translation without conveying the culturally accurate meaning, the result can range from misunderstanding to complete failure in communication and negotiations.

Voltaire, the great French political philosopher of the

eighteenth century, lamented the detrimental consequences of literal translations when he wrote:

Woe to the makers of literal translations, who by rendering every word weaken the meaning! It is indeed by so doing that we can say the letter kills and the spirit gives life.

This type of literal translation miscommunication is common between American and Asian companies and is one of the causes for why I stated in the previous chapter that the level of accuracy of communication in U.S.-Asian negotiations ranges only between seventy and ninety percent. This is true not only in the realm of business negotiating as we are discussing in this book but also in most areas of interaction, including the political relations between countries. In the previous chapter, we looked at the example of the miscommunication between the U.S president and the Japanese prime minister caused by literal translation.

> Literal translation miscommunication is common between American and Asian companies.

B.   THE USE OF IDIOMS

> "It's raining cats and dogs" leaves executives feeling totally perplexed.

The use of idioms also creates translation confusion and miscommunication. If a translator is not fully familiar with both cultures, then it will be impossible to correctly interpret the idioms that populate so many languages in the world.

By way of example, an American client used the phrase "it's raining cats and dogs" in a meeting in Osaka. In the U.S., the phrase would be understood to indicate a situation is very bad. As the translator was unfamiliar with this idiom, she had no other option but to translate it literally. When translated literally, that idiom leaves listeners either feeling totally perplexed, wondering if the American executive is still a little discombobulated from jetlag, or wanting to peer out the window to look at the sky to see what in the world is going on!

In another case, an executive of a Taipei firm was making a concession to the director of sales of my German client and said he would agree to the German company's position on a particular item if in return the German company would agree to meet a very specific production schedule for their orders. The director of sales replied: "That is fine. I will make sure that my company *leaves no stone unturned* in meeting that condition." While the Taiwanese were pleased with the first part of the answer, it was clear by the expressions on their faces that they were unsure what to make of the idiom in the answer's second part. During a subsequent coffee break, two executives pulled me over to the corner of the room and asked "Why was he talking about stones? We are negotiating about the medical device products that his company manufactures."

C. SAYING NO WITHOUT USING THE WORD "NO"

As already mentioned, there are approximately two dozen expressions in Japanese to say no, most of which have a literal meaning that has nothing to do with no. A list of these expressions even includes the word yes.

As we pointed out in the previous chapters, the many

ways to disagree come back to understanding the Japanese culture. According to their norms, disagreeing directly is considered impolite. Answering in the negative can create discord, which is contrary to group harmony. It is culturally correct, and indeed expected, that to maintain harmony, a speaker will use words other than saying "no" to indirectly express their lack of agreement or interest. This and other cultural impacts on communication in Japan are discussed in chapters three and four of this book.

D. DIFFERING BUSINESS CONCEPTS

Miscommunication and misunderstanding occur between American and Asian executives not only because of the different cultural meanings of *words* and *phrases* as we have just discussed but as a result of the different cultural meanings of *business concepts and actions* as well. Allow me to share an example.

> Miscommunication occurs not only because of the different cultural meanings of words but of business concepts and actions as well.

Early in my career in the course of setting up and managing an American client's business operations in Asia, my client and I developed a very strong working relationship with one Tokyo company in particular. We shall refer to the U.S. company as DE and to the Japanese company as PL. PL became very instrumental in our business in the Japan market. It conducted market research, helped introduce companies we could partner with, took care of obtaining regulatory approval to import and sell the products in Japan, and more. PL turned out to be an invaluable collaborator.

As the business grew, DE's CEO decided to establish a subsidiary in Tokyo. This would provide a strong market presence and direct, real-time access to all companies that DE was working with in Japan. The U.S. CEO wanted to invite the CEO of PL to become the honorary chairman of DE's Tokyo subsidiary. The reason, he explained, was to demonstrate our appreciation for the very strong business relationship between the two companies.

When I met with Mr. Bunno, PL's CEO, and extended DE's invitation to him, his whole countenance changed. He became very concerned and immediately turned down this invitation. I continued the meeting, discussing other topics. About forty-five minutes later, I again extended the invitation to him. He rejected it for a second time.

In keeping with the Japan custom to decline three times first and then accept an offer after it is presented the third time, I was confident that he would agree to the invitation after I asked a third time. Right before the meeting was to end, I extended the offer again for the third time, but Mr. Bunno's reply was the same. He adamantly rejected the invitation and did not subsequently say yes.

I was perplexed by this. Mr. Bunno was aware that the position was totally symbolic and did not require him to get involved in the affairs of the subsidiary in any way. The position was simply a token of appreciation of the good will between the two companies. So why was he saying no? After all, he had previously stated on several occasions how much he enjoyed working with DE and how much he admired DE's CEO.

After our meeting finished, we went to have dinner together.

Mr. Bunno loosened his tie after a few drinks. That is usually an excellent sign that a Japanese executive is relaxed and likely to talk more freely. Taking this cultural cue, I told Mr. Bunno that I was perplexed by his lack of interest in serving as honorary chairman of DE's Tokyo subsidiary. I reiterated that the position was totally honorary and that he would not be expected to become involved in the company's business affairs in any way. I added once again that the invitation was purely an expression of the good will and strong business relationship between the two companies.

Mr. Bunno looked away in silence for a few moments and then asked me how much DE's CEO wanted. I had no idea what he meant. He repeated, "How much does DE want?" When I still did not understand, Mr. Bunno went on to explain that in Japan asking someone to serve as an honorary executive is merely a polite way to ask that person to be become one of the major investors in that company. This, of course, was not DE's intent at all.

This is a clear example of how not only words and phrases but business concepts and actions can have totally different meanings across cultures. In the previous chapter we saw the different example of how the meaning of giving an executive a desk in front of a window is dissimilar to the meaning in the States.

II. IMPORTANCE OF AN IN-HOUSE INTERPRETER

Given the importance of a translator having cultural and language fluency for both countries, how can Americans know if the Asian company's native translator employee understands the American culture sufficiently to communicate intended messages between both parties? This is an especially critical question since U.S. executives usually only meet the Asian company's designated translator as the meeting begins. Not only is there no opportunity to confirm the translator's level of understanding of English and American culture but typically the Americans do not have anyone on their team who has the ability to confirm that level of understanding as well as the accuracy of translation. This leaves the U.S. executives in a precarious position and at a clear tactical disadvantage. It puts the very negotiation at risk.

> U.S. executives should want everyone representing and speaking for them to be in a position to understand and advance their corporate interests.

If the goal of a negotiation or business discussion is to advance a firm's corporate interests, then U.S. executives should want everyone representing and speaking for them to be in a position to understand and advance their corporate interests. This is another reason why U.S. companies need to have their own translator on their team.

Furthermore, during meetings, literally who speaks more than the translator? The fact of the matter is that in a business meeting that lasts two hours, assuming that the American and Asian executives speak for equal amounts of time—let's say thirty minutes each—the remaining hour is the time the translator needs to translate for both parties. From my own interpreting experience, I can report that the translator always speaks more than anyone else in a meeting. And on those occasions when a meeting takes place over a meal—such as a working lunch—the translator is kept busy during the whole lunch because he/she is constantly translating the conversational exchange with little, if any, opportunity to eat.

Not only does the translator have the most "talk time" during a meeting but also, whether intended or not, the translator often becomes the face and voice of the U.S. executives to their Asian counterparts and vice versa.

It is quite common for Asian executives to look at the translator located off to the side when they speak, even though the American executives they are having the discussion with are sitting directly across the table. In the case of Japan, there are two cultural factors that drive this communication dynamic:

- It is common for Japanese to feel uncomfortable speaking with foreigners so they naturally gravitate toward addressing the Japanese translator when talking and listening to foreigners. This offers them a greater level of comfort.

  I cannot recount the all too numerous occasions when, both in and outside of business meetings or situations, I would ask a question in proper Japanese and the Japanese person would look at and reply not to me, but to the Japanese person who happened to be with me. This stems from their lack of comfort interacting with non-Japanese, the consequence of being a homogenous society living on an island country isolated from the rest of the world throughout much of its history.

- In formal communication in Japanese culture, it is not polite to maintain continuous eye contact with the other party as we do in America. More information can be found on this in chapter four.

Interestingly enough, it is also common for American executives to look at the translator while addressing Asian counterparts. However, we do so for the exact opposite cultural reason.

In American culture, it is polite to maintain continuous eye contact with the person with whom you are speaking. So American executives look at the translator as they are speaking and then look at the Japanese while their words are being translated. As a result, it usually turns out that when the Americans are talking and looking at the translator, the Japanese are listening and looking at the Americans. Then when the Japanese are talking and looking at the translator, Americans are looking at the Japanese. The result is significantly less eye contact than if both parties were communicating in the same language. Not only is there less direct eye contact as a consequence of this dynamic, there is also a missed opportunity to fully read each other's body language, to communicate non-verbally, and to build a stronger mutual relationship.

If the goal of the meeting is to advance your corporate interests, then it is vital that the translator be a member of your team. For only if he or she is on your team can the translator:

- Know what your company's overall business interests are.

- Be aware of the specific goals your firm has for the negotiation.

- Be committed to your corporate interests.

- Have an interest in building your relationship with your Asian counterpart.

- Be in a position to actually promote your negotiating objectives and overall interests.

As mentioned already, American executives usually meet the translator at the time the meeting with the Asian company begins. In many cases, the translator is not even introduced to the foreign executives. In this circumstance, how much could the translator possibly know about the American company's business goals for this meeting? Likewise, the traditional translator has no commitment to or even interest in the American company's objectives and is not in any position to advance those business objectives. If the translator is an employee of the Asian company, then he or she will be interested in advancing the business interests of their company, not the U.S. company.

> The traditional translator has no commitment to or even interest in the American company's objectives.

Yet the unfortunate reality is that American companies go to meetings with Asian firms and almost never have a translator on their team. In contrast, the Asian businesses *always* prepare their own translator for their team. The result is that American companies are at a strategic and tactical disadvantage even before the negotiation's substantive discussions begin.

III. FACILITATOR: GOING BEYOND A TRANSLATOR

So far, this chapter has concentrated on the importance of proper cultural and linguistic translation skills as the key factors in

> U.S. companies need a facilitator interpreter, not just a traditional translator.

finding the right translator. Actually, the role of a good translator needs to be significantly broader if American companies wish to achieve their maximum success potential in global markets. U.S. companies need a *facilitator interpreter*, not just a traditional translator. They need someone who not only will provide accurate cultural translations of dialogue but also who will promote their interests by engaging in relationship building with Asian companies and advancing their strategic goals in negotiations and other business discussions.

In most cases, the translator is either an employee of the Asian company or is hired by them from an outside translation service. In the latter case, the translator is a third party to the meeting with zero prior knowledge of either the context or the content of the discussion. Furthermore, they have no vested interest in the negotiation's outcome. Their sole interest is to provide a correct literal translation of the dialogue. Corporate goals and strategic interests are unknown to these translators, particularly regarding the foreign company, and they could not care less about them.

> The result is that the contextual and strategic significance of what is being stated is usually not conveyed to the other party.

Further, translators hired from translation agencies often have no experience in the business world. Consequently, having no actual experience with or firsthand knowledge of what is being discussed, translators usually do not understand either the context or the implications of what is being communicated. This typically limits them to providing very narrow translations of the dialogue; they are unable to convey the larger meaning, implications, and intention of what is being discussed because they are simply not familiar with them. The result is that the contextual and strategic significance of what is being stated is usually not conveyed to the other party. The true intent of what the parties are trying to communicate gets quite literally "lost in translation" even though the translator may be fluent in both languages. One cannot fully and accurately convey what one does not fully and accurately comprehend.

Knowledge of a dictionary's meaning of a word alone is insufficient in fully communicating as well as advancing your company's interests. This is part of the reason I stated in the previous chapter that the level of accuracy in U.S.-Asian business translation typically ranges between seventy and ninety percent. I have observed meetings where the accuracy level was less than fifty percent.

Utilizing translators who are employees of the Asian company or of professional translation agencies does not advance the interests of an American company. Actually, it is a disadvantage to have them speak for your company. Instead, your company needs its own *facilitator interpreter* who will advance your corporate interests. The most desirable facilitator interpreter is effective in four distinct and critically important areas:

> The most desirable facilitator interpreter is effective in four distinct and critically important areas.

- **Correct linguistic translation:** Requiring thorough comprehension of both languages

- **Accurate and complete cultural interpretation:** Providing the actual cultural meaning as well as implication and expectation of what is being communicated as a part of the translation

- **Effective strategy development:** Helping ensure that negotiations and discussions secure your own corporate interests as well as the other party's

- **Relationship building:** Ensuring that the level of politeness, tone, protocol, content, and flow of the discussion are appropriate and aid in both establishing and strengthening the relationship with your Asian partner

  As discussed throughout this book, building and maintaining a favorable relationship is essential in succeeding in business in Asian markets.

In order to fulfill this essential role, the facilitator interpreter must be:

- A member of the American company's team—such as an employee or a consultant.

- Familiar with the U.S. company's business interests.

- Committed to achieving the American firm's corporate objectives.

- Able to effectively speak about and promote the U.S. company's interests.

- Vested in the outcome of the American company's interests and discussions.

- Fluent both linguistically and culturally in both American and the Asian country's culture.

- Experienced in relationship building and management in Asia.

In comparing a traditional translator to the facilitator interpreter that I advocate, a translator plays a two-dimensional role and contributes little to an American enterprise's business success. A translator can actually be an obstacle to your company's corporate goals as discussed above. On the other hand, a facilitator contributes through a three-dimensional role and is in a position to make major contributions to advancing your company's business success.

> A translator plays a two-dimensional role, and a facilitator contributes through a three-dimensional role.

To express the difference between a traditional translator and a facilitator interpreter, I use the analogy that a translator is comparable to a tollbooth clerk who collects tolls on a road while the facilitator is comparable to a traffic officer who directs the flow of traffic on that same road.

A tollbooth clerk has no interest in where your car has come from or where it is going. His only concern is to get your car from one side of the tollbooth to the other. In the same way, translators have no interest in where an American company is coming from strategically or where the company and the negotiations are going; they simply want to get the discussions to go from the start of the meeting to its finish.

As a result, a translator allows literal translations to pass between companies from one side of the negotiating table to the other. He or she is not concerned about how literal translations impact both parties or how the parties might react. Furthermore, the translator has no vested interest in how well the meeting goes or in the negotiation's outcome. Finally, the translator has no interest in relationship building between the two companies.

In contrast, the traffic officer directs the flow of traffic to help you get where you need to go. If you put your left turn signal on, he will stop the oncoming traffic in the opposite direction so you can make that left turn. When you need to make a right turn, the traffic officer will stop pedestrian traffic so you can make that turn. In this way, the traffic officer knows your intentions and helps you move in the direction you want—smoothly and with as little obstruction as possible. Likewise, the well-prepared facilitator interpreter will help an American company achieve its corporate objectives by appropriately guiding the direction of the meeting, the flow of the discussion, and the relationship building between both companies. In addition, the facilitator interpreter is in a position to ensure that proper cultural norms are maintained throughout the discussions.

If a U.S. company relies on the Asian company to provide a translator who ends up being their employee, that translator will act to facilitate the interests of the Asian company, not the interests of the American company. It is critically important for U.S. executives to have a facilitator interpreter on their own team.

Another example of the critical role of the facilitator interpreter can be seen when using the services of an attorney. When preparing an international sales agreement, joint venture agreement, or patent agreement, it is a matter of course that a company always has their own attorney represent their firm and does not rely on the attorney of the other company. That is standard operating procedure and is done to best secure their strategic interests. It would be foolish not to do so. In the same way, prudence dictates that American executives have their own facilitator interpreter who is aware of, committed to, and able to promote their corporate interests when negotiating.

To share a lengthy but vivid example, the executive assistant to the president of a Japanese sales company, in expressing appreciation, sent me a description of the added value I contributed as a facilitator interpreter in her company's dealings with one of my clients. I share this full letter with you to provide an illustration of the importance of a facilitator interpreter from the viewpoint of my American client's partner in Tokyo.

> *I really appreciate Mr. Azar's participation since he has facilitated our business process by interpreting our conversation in the way which cultural difference between US and Japan would not become an obstacle between us. Without him our business would have to go through a lot more difficulties due to the cultural differences.*
>
> *I often translate for the president of my company. So*

one time I discussed translating with Mr. Azar. I was surprised to hear him say that it is quite important for an interpreter to be acquainted with different cultures and take the cultural difference into consideration. Being acquainted with American, Japanese and other Asian cultures, Mr. Azar does not only interpret our conversation but also adds necessary information if needed so that the true message can be conveyed without misunderstanding.

For example, last month my boss handed a gift to the President & CEO of one of our American business partners at the beginning of our meeting and said in Japanese "tsumaranai-mono desuga" (つまらないものですが). A literal translation of these words would be "Though this is a worthless thing."

I can imagine no one would be pleased by receiving something worthless. This is one of the typical Japanese expressions used very often. As modesty is considered a virtue in Japanese society, Japanese people tend to use expressions which may sound too self-deprecating to non-Japanese if the expression is interpreted literally.

A hidden message of this expression is: "Perhaps this gift is not precious or valuable at all for such a well-off and noble person like you, but I chose the most valuable and beautiful thing I could find hoping that you would like it." At that time Mr. Azar interpreted this expression as the following: "In accord with the Japanese custom, we would like to start today's meeting by offering our humble gift as an expression of our gratitude for this opportunity to work together." I was really impressed by his interpretation.

If he had interpreted the expression literally, our business partner would have wondered why my boss had brought something worthless as a gift. Had he explained the hidden message of this expression, it would have been too long and sounded too self-deprecatory to Americans. However, his interpretation was perfect. He interpreted the phrase "a worthless thing" into "our humble gift" to express the modesty of my boss properly, he also added the information that it is a Japanese custom to give a gift to business partners, and at the end he clearly conveyed the true message of my boss even though it was not mentioned (by my boss) at all.

Grammatically speaking, there was no main clause in the phrase "Though this is a worthless thing." It was only a subordinate clause. I usually cannot interpret such Japanese sentences into English so I would have asked my boss what the main clause was. Actually the missing main clause was "We give you this gift as an expression of our gratitude (though this is a worthless thing)." The most important message of my boss was "as an expression of our gratitude" though he didn't mention it.

Not only my boss but also most Japanese tend to express their intention with only a few words. This is probably because people can understand each other without explaining everything in an almost homogeneous society where we share the same culture. I am often frustrated by this tendency when I try to translate my boss' words into English. In many cases, subjects, verbs or objectives are omitted from his words. So I need to figure out what the missing words are, find an appropriate expression in English to convey the true intention, and incorporate it to the translation. It requires a lot of time for me. Mr. Azar does the same process instantly at our meetings.

Being familiar with both cultures, he has converted a typical Japanese expression into an appropriate English expression, added the information needed, and most importantly, conveyed its true message. He did all these things at the instant of hearing my boss' words. This is why I greatly admire Mr. Azar as an excellent facilitator of our mutual business. Needless to say, our business partner was delighted with the gift my boss brought, and the meeting went well following the wonderful start in a warm atmosphere. This is all due to his exquisite interpretation. — **Kawahara Emiko, Executive Assistant to the President, Shimizu, Inc.**

Given the critically important role of the facilitator interpreter, it is truly astonishing how little attention U.S. companies give to it. By failing to take advantage of a facilitator's value, they unilaterally give up all of the benefits the facilitator brings and place themselves at a strategic and tactical disadvantage relative to their Asian counterparts who invariably have their own translator. And this disadvantage is locked in even before the negotiation commences. Companies will find that the cost of a facilitator is well worth the expense.

There are two ways an American company can have a facilitator interpreter on their team. One is to hire such an individual as an employee and the other is to retain their services as an outside consultant. As always, it is prudent to execute a non-disclosure agreement with any party your company will be sharing confidential and strategic information with. This is especially important given that the greater the individual's understanding of

> Given the critically important role of the facilitator interpreter, it is truly astonishing how little attention U.S. companies give to it.

your firm, its overall business goals, and your specific strategic objectives for the Asian market targeted, the more effective the facilitator interpreter can be. Likewise, the greater the period of time and the degree of involvement in your business, the more effective the facilitator interpreter is in a position to be.

IV. HOW FLUENT IS FLUENT

Translators who are on the staff of the local company involved in the meeting as well as those who are employed by professional translation agencies are not the only ones who can be an obstacle to the success of American companies in international markets. For example, non-native Asian speakers employed by American companies who present themselves as being fluent in Asian languages can be an even greater hindrance to success in those markets.

As we know, it is rare to find Americans who speak Asian languages with sufficient proficiency to be able to conduct business in them. Often American business men and women claim they are "fluent" in a foreign language when in fact they are only able to carry on basic social conversation. The following is a brief example of how detrimental the results can be when an employee inaccurately claims to be fluent in an Asian language and U.S. companies hire them assuming they are fluent.

An American company's expectation that Japan should be their largest global market was not borne out by their sales results. Realizing they needed help to raise bottom line revenue from their Japan operation, the company wanted a new director of international sales who was fluent in Japanese. They hired an individual who claimed on his resume and during the interview process that he was. When I started working with him, however, it became clear that his spoken Japanese was not up to conducting business in Japanese nor could he read or write the language. This lack of facility brought serious consequences to the company, costing it tens of millions of dollars in lost sales, time, and expenses that were completely avoidable.

Here are two other circumstances in which the matter of "how fluent is fluent" is relevant to succeeding in communicating in international markets. The first concerns non-native speakers of Asian languages who actually are proficient in them. Allow me to share a firsthand experience I had early on in my career to illustrate this point.

At that time, I worked on Wall Street as a financial analyst and political economist in the North American headquarters of Japan's second largest brokerage house, Daiwa Securities, Inc., located in the World Financial Center on Wall Street. Shortly after joining the firm, it was announced that the company's CEO would be visiting from the corporate headquarters in Osaka. As he did not speak English, I was asked to interpret his speech to all 540 employees. It was an honor to be asked.

The appointed day arrived and I was on the stage with the CEO. When he started to speak, I immediately realized that he was speaking the Osaka dialect of the Japanese language. I froze and turned as red as a tomato. He noticed this, but he did not understand what was happening and continued speaking in that dialect. The president of the North American headquarters, who recognized what was going on, immediately ran up on stage and, smiling at me, said: "Don't worry. I'll take care of this." I was mortified. While I speak standard Japanese, which is Tokyo dialect, I am not conversant in Osaka dialect.

UK English and American English are much the same but do have notable differences, and there are small colloquial differences across the country in the U.S. However, the differences between dialects in Asian countries tend to be much more significant. To illustrate this point, let's look at a quick example of a difference between standard Japanese (Tokyo dialect) and Osaka dialect for the greeting "How are you?"

- In standard Japanese, the phrase is *ogenki desuka* (お元気ですか) and the literal meaning is "Are you well?"

- In Osaka dialect, the phrase is *mokari makka* (もかりまっか) and the literal meaning is "Are you making money?"

Two entirely different phrases with very different literal

meanings have the same cultural meaning within their respective dialects. The same situation exists in China which, depending on how they are classified, has over two hundred dialects. This is another example of the prevalence of words and phrases whose actual cultural meaning has no relation to its literal meaning.

While most Japanese speak standard Japanese, local dialects are still used and can be problematic for non-native speakers of Japanese who are fluent in standard Japanese.

A second case regarding "how fluent is fluent" involves native speakers of Asian languages. While a native translator might be fluent in English as well as their own native tongue, there are times when they are not familiar with the specialized terminology that often comes up in negotiations and other business meetings and presentations. They need to be familiar with the specialized terminology in both languages to translate accurately.

The parallel situation that we commonly experience in America is when a doctor discusses a medical condition in medical terms. The patient and their family who are hearing the information for the first time often need to ask the doctor to explain what was said in lay terms. While the specialized terminology is obviously part of their native language, the patient and family often do not understand what the medical terms mean without special training.

This potential terminology risk in translation is problematic in the case of employee translators as well as translators hired from professional translation agencies. Problematic terminology translation is another cause of the compromised accuracy in negotiation communication mentioned earlier in this book. If it is necessary to hire translators, American executives need to confirm that both the translation agency and the individual translator(s) that the American company hires are experienced in the company's field of specialization. For presentations, give the translation agency the presentation at least two weeks in advance of the meeting date

This potential terminology risk in translation is problematic.

so they can make sure they are familiar with all of the specialized terminology.

Another client experience occurred when I was establishing a business in Japan for an American maker of specialty medical skin care products. We selected the Japanese company we wanted to partner with, and they were engaging in a due diligence review of the product ingredients for regulatory approval. The head of their regulatory affairs department also happened to be their medical skin care product expert. She had over twenty years of experience and was exceptionally talented at what she did.

One of the product ingredients was ornithine, an amino acid that produces powerful anti-aging benefits. The problem was that no one on the regulatory review team at the company was familiar with the word, and it was not in any of the dictionaries available to them, neither standard dictionaries nor scientific ones. The closest word in any of the Japanese dictionaries was ornithology, the study of birds. As a result, the regulatory team mistakenly concluded that the ingredient was a derivative of bird dung. You can imagine the surprise my client's president and I had when we received a fax from the president of the Japanese sales company saying they feared that they would not be able to obtain Japanese government approval for our products because they contained bird poop!

> Any American company that wants to maximize success in international markets must have their own in-house facilitator interpreter.

This experience reinforces the need for American companies to have their own in-house language expert who is in a position to determine the correct translations for specialized terminology.

As this chapter makes clear, any American company that wants to maximize success and minimize risk and expense in international markets must have their own in-house facilitator interpreter. Utilizing only a traditional translator will shortchange the efforts of any Western company engaging in business internationally. Even if they are able to provide accurate literal and cultural interpretation, they are not in a position to advance your strategic interests and bottom line goals.

INSIGHTS

As Anthony Burgess stated, "Translation is not a matter of words only: it is a matter of making intelligible a whole culture." This could not apply more to the world of international business, and it applies exponentially to intercultural negotiating. And, obviously, no one plays a greater role in translation than the translator. Hence, the translator plays a critically important role in international negotiating.

Achieving maximum success in international negotiating requires, as this chapter demonstrates, the translator to transcend simply translating the words of negotiation dialogue. The reason is that so often literal translations have nothing to do with actual meaning and intentions in international markets. Hearing only the correct dictionary translation is insufficient for fully advancing the business interests of American executives. On the contrary, literal translations can be a disservice because they lead to miscommunication, misunderstanding, incorrect expectations, and mistaken conclusions about where the negotiation stands and what is next.

Based on my experience, the translator's function must be viewed as being more than the translating of the negotiation dialogue. To be effective, it is imperative that the translator promote comprehensive and accurate communication. This is done through the following two means:

- Explaining the actual cultural meaning, business ramifications, and implied expectations of what is communicated

- Including in their translations what is omitted by Asian executives due to cultural norms of politeness but is nonetheless important for American executives to know

U.S. companies are significantly more likely to achieve maximum long-term success in negotiating in Asia when, going beyond language interpretation, the translator is also able to facilitate that central and critically important dimension of Asian negotiating—relationship building. Promoting the specific goals for the negotiation and the overall business interests of American executives is likewise needed. As illustrated in the analogy of the traffic officer, the skilled facilitator interpreter can be very effective in promoting strategy development and success optimization for your firm.

Who can fulfill these central and diverse functions? A traditional translator cannot. Only a *facilitator interpreter* can. And it is crucial for American companies to have their own in-house facilitator interpreter on their negotiating team.

PART THREE

ADDITIONAL STRATEGIES FOR SUCCESS

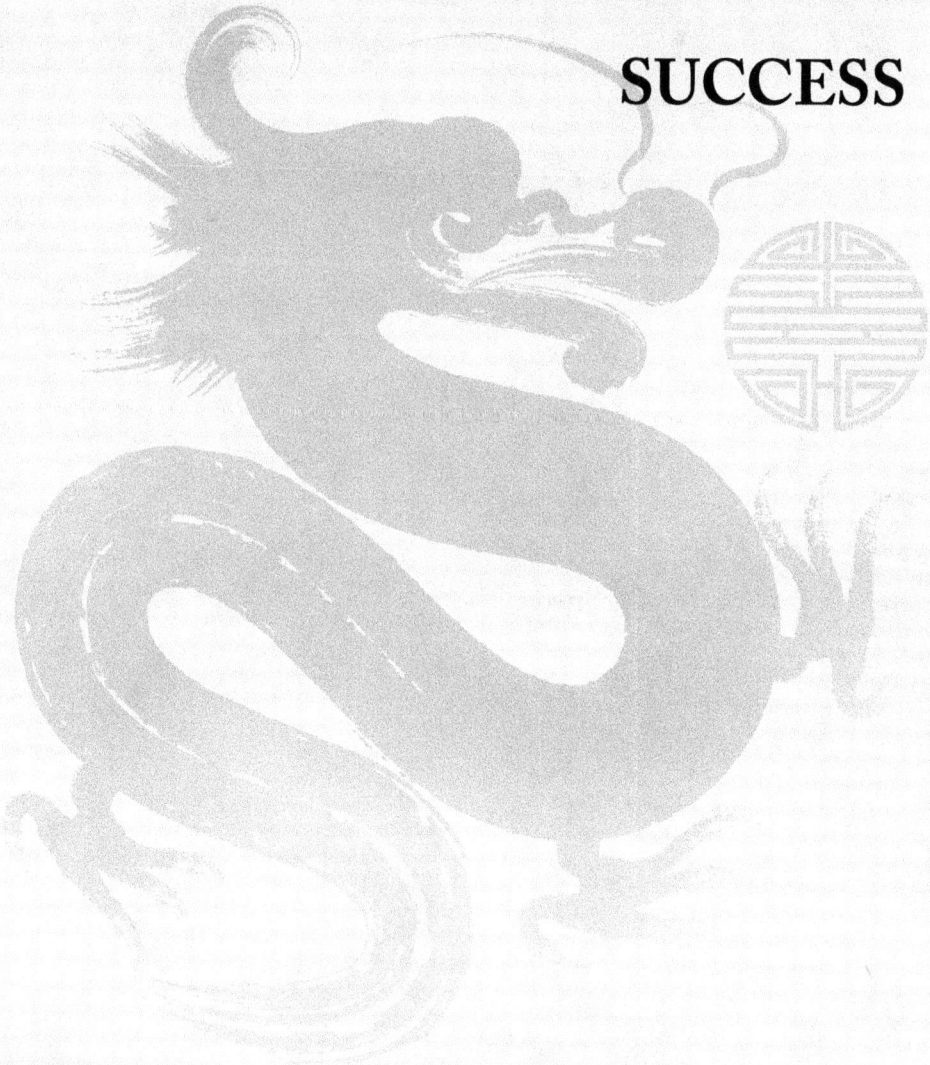

CHAPTER 6

FURTHER NEGOTIATION
CONSIDERATIONS

I. YOUR MOST IMPORTANT PIECE OF LUGGAGE

When you pack for your trip to Asia to negotiate with potential business partners, you will prepare two or more pieces of luggage. When considered from the perspective of how you can maximize the success of your negotiations there, however, your most important piece of luggage is the one that you do *not* bring with you.

Let's step back for a minute. One of the most fundamental mistakes I have witnessed American and European clients make over the years is the assumption that their way of negotiating—and engaging in business in general—will serve them well in Asia. After all, they are well-seasoned executives with notable track records of success. They are among their firm's best. Their approach has yielded significant success, and their tactics and techniques have served them well in negotiations for years. Often this is the only negotiating method they know, and it does not occur to them to consider there are other methods.

As we have seen throughout this book, however, negotiating in Asia and negotiating in America are profoundly different. Everything from the purpose, the goal, the approach, the dynamics, and even the requirements of negotiating are dissimilar. In short, the road to succeeding in negotiating in Asia is quite a different road than the one that successful American companies have travelled down in the States.

For example, as a consequence of the numerous factors examined throughout this entire book, the speed limits that are observed on the road of negotiation are very different—faster in America, much slower in Asia. The road contours are likewise dissimilar—direct in the U.S. with our linear logic and straight-forward approach versus winding and rambling in Asia where a holistic negotiating mindset requires taking an integrated view along the scenic route the parties need to travel as they incorporate not only the specifics of the business under discussion but also the varied and complex requirements of relationship building and greater mutual interests.

As the roads of successful negotiating are different in these two geographic areas, the U.S. map to successful negotiating is often not an effective guide to negotiating in Asia. Would any one expect a road map of Boston to be effective in getting them where they want to go in Bangkok, Shanghai, Singapore, or Seoul? In the same way, assuming that what works in

U.S. negotiations will bring positive results in Asia or any other foreign markets is a profound miscalculation in international negotiating and business in general. Accordingly, it is highly advisable that American executives neither pack nor bring with them to any international market the luggage of the approach they used when negotiating in their home market.

> Assuming that what works in U.S. negotiations will bring positive results in Asia is a profound miscalculation in international negotiating

Instead, I recommend that U.S. companies start out with the stance that everything they know about negotiating and conducting business from their experience in their home market will not be appropriate in international markets. Once they are actually working in-country in the target market, let their experience there, the direct feedback from the market, and the input they receive from experts on the local market such as consultants, mentors, partners, peers, and their in-house facilitator interpreter confirm what in their previous experience can be successfully utilized in each individual global market. This approach will best enable executives to ascertain the negotiating methods that are most appropriate for and effective in each market. This mindset is one of the most important pieces that executives should pack for their negotiation trips.

II. NEGOTIATING THE RIGHT PRODUCTS

It is common for businesses to adopt a cookie-cutter approach regarding which products to sell when expanding into foreign markets. However, that one-size-fits-all approach is not appropriate for every international market a company seeks to enter. Executives tend to think that their current best-selling product will be a best seller in each international market. While this can be true some of the time, it is not true all of the time. In my experience, it is not uncommon for a client's best-selling product in America or Europe to fail to achieve that status in Asia—indeed, sometimes that product hardly sold at all.*

So, which of its many products should a company choose to negotiate for best sales results as it embarks on expanding into international markets? This is a critical decision that needs to be carefully considered as executives formulate both their market entry and long-term business strategies for each country. There are several market conditions and cultural factors that should go into determining which products to sell in each individual market. These include the following eight specific factors:

A. REGULATORY CONSIDERATIONS

The time and cost for applying for regulatory approval from Asian governments to import and sell foreign products varies from country to country and industry to industry from a few months to several years and from a few thousand dollars to millions of dollars. The time to clarify the regulatory circumstances of products and decide on an optimal regulatory strategy is at the outset of negotiating and market entry. A well-qualified local partner in each country or an industry consultant will be able to assist with this.

---

* For a detailed analysis of the numerous factors that should be included in a company's product selection decisions for international markets, see chapter eight in *Navigating Japan's Business Culture* by Robert Charles Azar.

Failure to effectively manage a target market's regulatory issues up front can cost U.S. companies years of time and millions of dollars. Regulatory considerations should be among the first items American executives take care of—this point cannot be emphasized enough. If a potential local partner is not effective in your efforts to determine your firm's regulatory status and strategy in their market that is a definite red flag; it is an indication that they are not an appropriate partner and you should eliminate them from consideration.

An additional concern here is that regulatory approval may require product redesign, reformulation, or reconstitution. Such changes may have a negative impact on the product's performance and effectiveness or even result in a completely different product that may or may not meet market expectations.

There are instances where a best-selling foreign product might require considerably more time and cost to earn approval than a company's less popular product. Executives need to weigh whether it makes sense to start with those secondary products while the company's best-selling products are still undergoing government approval for sale in the future.

A regulatory review of a company's best-selling product may even determine that the product cannot be sold in a given international market due to prohibitive redevelopment costs or time-to-market delays or because so many product alterations would be needed to meet government requirements that the product would no longer be effective in providing its intended benefits.

B. MARKET DEMAND FOR MULTIPLE PRODUCT CATEGORIES

> There are occasions where one of a firm's secondary product categories experiences greater demand in Asia than its primary product category.

When American manufacturers have more than one product category, demand for their best-selling product category may not necessarily be as strong in Asian countries as in other markets. There are occasions where one of a firm's secondary product categories experiences greater demand there than its primary product category. In that case, executives need to decide whether or not it would make sense to make their secondary category products the main products in those markets and negotiate with local companies that would be appropriate for those products. Asian companies suited to selling your best-selling U.S. product category may not necessarily be the best for handling other product categories of your firm. Likewise, your secondary product category items may sell better in different sales channels than your leading product category items.

C. SELECTING PRODUCTS FROM WITHIN THE BEST-SELLING CATEGORY

It is common for U.S. companies to research the competitive standing of their best-selling products abroad to understand how those products might fare in international markets. However, rather than taking it for granted that those leading products in its best-selling category will be the company's best performers overseas, the company should analyze their other products in that same best-selling product category to see how they fare. It could turn out that a lower or even much lower ranking product in the States is a more appealing product abroad than that best-seller from the American market.

In the experience of one client, the manufacturer of a leading dermatological laser in the States, their best-selling laser turned out to be too large for the much smaller operating rooms typical in their target Asian market. However, the much smaller and portable demo unit that I used to demonstrate the lasers to clinics across the country was appropriately scaled for the conditions of

> It could turn out that a lower ranking product in the States is a more appealing product abroad than that best-seller from the American market.

that country. While not offering the full range of capabilities as the full-sized product, the demo unit version still incorporated the company's unique technology and enough advantages over competing products in the market that it became the company's best-selling product in Asia's largest dermatological laser market.

This experience is another example of:

- How what works in the U.S. does not necessarily bring success in international markets.

- How it is not always the best-selling product in America that produces the best sales results, captures the most market share, and establishes the strongest brand leadership for U.S. firms in overseas markets.

D. STRENGTHS OF YOUR ASIAN PARTNER

Within each international market, potential business partners will have their own different strengths and weaknesses. American executives need to analyze both when assessing potential partner companies during negotiations. It can be anticipated that any given company is better suited to sell certain products of a U.S. company's complete product line than other companies. This is due to several factors including the following seven:

- The Asian company's resources

- Their standing in their respective industry

- Their strength in their specific product categories

- Their strength in each of the sales channels your products have the potential to be sold in

- The degree of their nationwide distribution and sales capability

- The geographic appropriateness of their nationwide distribution and sales capability for your specific products—specifically, whether their customer base represents the largest and most appropriate group of potential product users

- Their strength in working with the most appropriate product spokesperson, if applicable

As a result, partner selection can also impact which products it makes sense to focus on in each international market. There are occasions where those products are not the ones executives originally had identified for that market.

E.   INFLUENCE OF SALES CHANNELS

Like most major markets, Asian countries have numerous major sales channels. These channels include the following:

- Traditional wholesale and retail channels

- Discount sales channel

- Medical channel

- Direct marketing sales channel—advertisements with toll free telephone numbers in newspapers and magazines, inserts, pamphlets, etc.

- Internet sales

- Television shopping

- Network marketing

Product sales volumes can vary greatly depending on the sales channels where they are sold. Products may end up needing to be sold in one channel as opposed to another as a result of the foreign company's preference, regulatory guidelines, market requirements, pricing, or the experience of the Asian partner and that will greatly influence sales channel strategy as well as product selection strategy.

> Succeeding in sales channels with lower sales volume potential can yield greater total sales volume in the long term.

In the event a U.S. company's products can be sold in more than one sales channel, American executives may not want to automatically select the channel likely to result in the greatest sales volume at the outset. Succeeding in certain sales channels with lower sales volume potential initially can yield greater total sales volume in the long term by establishing your company's corporate identity, brand image, and market leadership in the local market. Once established, these strengths can be transferred to other sales channels, producing greater sales volumes than otherwise would have been possible.

For example, if products can be sold in both the medical and retail channels, it is often better to commence sales in the medical channel even though it is expected to have smaller sales potential. Success in the medical channel establishes a high level of credibility for a company, its brand, and its product, which cannot be attained in retail channels. Once branding and credibility are attained in the medical channel that credibility and market leadership can be transferred to other sales channels, often resulting in even greater sales volume than would have been possible entering those non-medical sales channels first. With appropriate products, this approach strengthens a foreign company's market share not only in the short term but over the long term as well.

Conversely, products that succeed in the retail channel first and then are launched in the medical channel generally do not do as well in either channel. The primary reason for this is that physicians are skeptical of the clinical efficacy of products that become popular as retail products. Products categorized as medical products require a manufacturer to provide proof of a significantly greater level of clinical results than is necessary for retail channel products. Therefore, the clinical efficacy of products made by retail product makers is often questioned by physicians and the public.

F. CONSUMER PREFERENCES

In addition to regulatory requirements, U.S. products often need to be modified to meet consumer preferences in Asian markets. Three representative product preference examples include:

(1) **Product size.** Different markets prefer different sizes of the same products. In the States, for example, we tend to like bigger products. The option consumers have to supersize their order is ubiquitous in America. This is not the case in Asia. The Japanese market, for example, is at the other end of the size preference spectrum, requiring products that are sized smaller than in most other countries. There are two major reasons for this:

- Japanese are well known for their penchant for miniaturization—think of their centuries' old tradition of creating sculpted dwarf bonsai trees or how they revolutionized electronics, IT, and so many other industries by first miniaturizing vacuum tubes into transistors, allowing small size TVs, radios, computers, and later developing memory chips that made the IT revolution and so many other products possible.

- Another reason for their preference for small-scaled products is the practical consideration that Japan is significantly space constrained. A very mountainous area smaller than the state of California is home to Japan's population of 127 million people—a population equal to about forty percent of America's population. As much as ninety percent of the land is uninhabitable being too mountainous, resulting in very high population density and smaller homes, offices, cars, and roads.

Many foreign products such as cars, office equipment, furniture, and home appliances are simply too big for the conditions of the Japanese market. In addition, cultural differences and preferences once again come into play. For example, Japanese prefer to buy their family's food fresh every day, so they buy in small quantities and have no need for the large refrigerators common in the States. In addition, U.S. refrigerators are simply too large to fit in most kitchens in that nation.

(2) **Product features**. Consumer demands and expectations for a product's performance will dictate what features a product must have. As is true in any international market, products must meet the specific market needs of targeted Asian countries if they are to sell well there.

(3) **Fragrance:** Unlike consumers in the West who enjoy fragranced products, Japanese prefer fragrance neutral (fragrance free) products.

G. NUMBER OF PRODUCTS—THE SHARPSHOOTER APPROACH

In the event a foreign company has a large product line, it is advisable to enter international markets with a select few products initially, rather than most of or the entire product line at once, and then add more products over time. Taking this sharpshooter rather than shotgun approach allows U.S. firms and their Asian partners to focus on, monitor, manage, and maximize their product sales with greater efficiency and effectiveness.

> It is advisable to enter international markets with a select few products initially, rather than the entire product line at once.

This sharpshooter product selection approach generally yields yet another important benefit. Launching in Asian markets with fewer rather than a greater number of product SKUs and then adding products as the first products become established usually results in greater success in establishing a foreign company's market share and brand leadership.

H. CULTURAL TRANSLATABILITY

In order to succeed in an international market, the names of the U.S. company and its products need to translate well culturally in that foreign market. Likewise, any marketing slogans need to be checked for cultural appropriateness.

To cite a few examples:

> The names of the U.S. company and its products need to translate well culturally in that foreign market.

The company name "Best Buy" in Chinese is *bai si mai* (百思买). Meaning "to buy after thinking 100 times," this name tells potential customers that they must work very hard to decide what to buy in that store—not the most inviting name to draw customers in to shop.

The initial Chinese rendition of Kentucky Fried Chicken's "Finger-lickin' good" was "Eat your fingers off."

The first translation of Coca-Cola in Chinese was pronounced *ke-kou-kela* and meant "bite the wax tadpole."

Pepsi Cola did not fare any better; the translation in Taiwan for its early slogan "Come alive with the Pepsi Generation" was "Pepsi will bring our ancestors back from the dead."

Clairol, the popular hair care products manufacturer, sold their "Mist Stick" curling iron in Germany without realizing that in German slang mist means manure.

When Schweppes Tonic Water was first introduced into the Italian market, the Italian translation meant Schweppes Toilet Water. Italians do not particularly care to drink toilet water. An additional point of market confusion: Is "toilet water" a drink or a light perfume?

This cultural translatability problem of company and product names is huge and has the potential to limit or outright destroy success potential in international markets.

The challenge of cultural translatability, however, is not limited to U.S. companies selling abroad. Foreign companies entering the American market stumble over the same problem. Electrolux, the Scandinavian maker of vacuum cleaners, launched their business in the States with the marketing slogan "Nothing sucks like an Electrolux." When Japan's top-tier Otsuka Pharmaceutical Company launched "Calpis," a blockbuster sports drink in their domestic market, in the States, its name was mistakenly adopted and pronounced as "cow piss." Is it any wonder that sales of these products suffered due to these cultural blunders until they were remedied?

The problem of cultural translatability does not apply only to the names of companies and products. The names of company executives can likewise have undesirable meanings as discussed in section IV of this chapter.

III. SELECTING THE RIGHT COMPANIES FOR YOUR NEGOTIATIONS

A. SCREENING AND SELECTING THE RIGHT PARTNER

When American companies seek to enter a foreign market, there are often several potential partners that they will meet with to negotiate and make their partner selection. How can they effectively screen, evaluate, and select the most appropriate local business partner in Asia markets, and what criteria should U.S. executives use in that effort? Here are fifteen major criteria that should be considered:

(1) **The history of the Asian company:** It is important to research the company's track record. How long has the company been in business and how successful have they been in meeting their goals?

(2) **Experience and capabilities:** Regardless of how long a company has been operating, it is necessary to study the company's length, depth, and breadth of experience in their particular industry, sales channel, and product category. For example, one former client was interested in partnering with a large Beijing-based corporation that was presenting themselves as a strong potential partner in their domestic market. In conducting due diligence for my client, I discovered that the company became successful by manufacturing batteries and had no experience or inroads in my client's industry. Their strategic goal was to use my client's business as the opportunity to enter my client's industry.

It is important to determine a potential partner's actual capabilities and possible weaknesses. For example, does the company sell directly to the end-users of your product or do they need to go through intermediaries? Obviously, selling directly to product end-users is most favorable. Depending on the particulars, an Asian company's selling to end-users through one intermediary sales company can be unproblematic, but generally speaking a potential partner company's need for multiple intermediaries is not desirable and should be viewed as a potential red flag.

(3) **Financial performance:** What is the company's overall financial condition? Review the company's track record for sales and profitability over the past five to ten years.

(4) **Corporate culture and management strategy:**

Within any industry, every company has its own corporate culture and management strategy. This is true of most international markets. American executives should determine to what degree the prospective partner's culture and strategy align with their own.

For instance, if a U.S. company's strategic objectives for an international market include establishing the company, brand, and product as an industry leader there, is the potential partner likewise interested in that goal? Is the potential partner experienced in achieving that goal? Or, in contrast, are they a "flavor of the month" type of company solely interested in selling as many units of your product as they can for as long as sales are strong but then moving on to other business projects if or when sales weaken? Even more problematic, does their history and reputation indicate that they are willing to "push the envelope" and engage in actions that are gray area activities, outright questionable, or that skirt existing or expected laws and regulations governing your industry and product?

(5) **Industry standing:** Whenever possible, seek out top tier prospects for potential partnerships. What is the company's standing in their industry? Obviously, the greater a company's standing in their industry, the more they are likely to be able to bring to your business and, consequently, the stronger a partner they are likely to be. While there sometimes are exceptions, as a general rule, it is not advisable to work with a company that is not in the top tier of their industry.

The Korean market presents an interesting situation in this regard that American executives need to be aware of. Despite the fact that eighty percent of Korea's economy is dominated by its four major conglomerates, there are many industries in which small- and mid-sized firms are the major players. One example is the medical skin care industry. It is noteworthy that when these smaller companies present themselves to U.S. companies seeking their business in Korea, they all claim to be number one in their industry. According to them, there is no number two or three. Every Korean company that approaches an American company states that it is number one in their domestic industry! That math obviously does not add up, and American companies need to investigate prospective partner companies thoroughly before commencing with negotiations and working together.

(6) **Industry reputation:** While industry standing is a measurable level of a company's achievement for things such as sales revenues or market share, industry reputation is how a company is perceived and thought of by others in the industry and society at large. For example, how is the company regarded by fellow professionals in that industry? Does the company have a reputation for conducting business in a professional, legal, and ethical manner, or are they known for cutting corners, engaging in questionable business practices, and stealing the intellectual property of foreign firms?

Such unprofessional dealings can be extremely costly to an American company. Allow me to cite the experience of a former client before they engaged my consulting services. A world leader in medical skin care products, they entered into a multimillion dollar joint venture with a pharmaceutical company in the world's largest skin care market. While the American company was not aware of the pharmaceutical company's reputation, it was well known in the local market that they had a history of being unethical in their practices, including stealing the intellectual property of overseas companies. That is exactly what happened—the joint venture turned out to be a sham to obtain the American company's world-leading technology, and the pharmaceutical company launched a knock off of the American company's product. It was at that point that I began working with the American company to get them out of their dilemma and relaunch in the most important market in the world for their product.

(7) **Spokesperson collaboration:** In the event that sales of your company's products can be enhanced by utilizing a spokesperson such as a celebrity, sports player, or physician, you need to ascertain if a potential international partner has a track record of attracting and working with the right spokespersons.

If the leading spokespersons in your industry in an Asian market do not work with a company that is interested in your business, this is definitely a red flag. Likewise, the caliber of the spokespersons who do work with the partner company is indicative of that company's standing and reputation in their market. For example, if a company's spokesperson for a medical product is not a first tier, recognized authority physician, that is a red flag.

(8) **Sufficient financial resources:** A potential international partner company should possess sufficient financial resources to market, sell, and provide after-sales customer care and maintenance to the level of the American company's satisfaction. Equally important to *possessing* sufficient financial resources, are they *committing* the requisite resources—financial and others?

(9) **Appropriate sales plan:** Consider how likely a potential partner's business plans are to attain your desired goals for their market. Are their plans likely to achieve the expected level of sales? Are their plans likely to advance your standing and

reputation in the international market? Furthermore, does the company have successful experience executing the sales activities included in its business plan for your company? U.S. firms can access this information from appropriate industry consultants, market research firms, and government agencies.

(10) **Corporate commitment:** While capital is a major factor, it is not the only commitment factor to consider when assessing a company's commitment to the partnership. A more complete list would include the following four items:

- Number of employees they are committing to the business

- Number of company departments or divisions that will be involved

- Number of affiliates in the case of large corporations; in the case of small- and medium-sized firms, the number of cooperating companies

- Number of years in the company's plan for the business project included *within* your business agreement with them—one year, three years, five years

As we have discussed, Asian companies engage in business with a long-term orientation. Accordingly, a top-tier company will have a plan for your business for *beyond* the time period specified in most business agreements. Discussing this with a potential partner company provides American executives with a much clearer understanding of the local company's level of interest and commitment.

For example, what is their internal company outlook for your business in years four and five? This is critically important to ascertain as the greater their long-term intentions are, the greater their investment and activity for your business will be in the short- and midterm as well—in other words, for the first two or three years specified in your business agreement with them. Conversely, if a potential partner company does not have a longer-term outlook for your business, that is a definite sign of low priority interest in your business and usually is an indication that they are not a major player in their industry.

(11) **Exclusive or non-exclusive business agreement:** A foreign company's insistence on having exclusive rights in its business agreement with your company is a major indicator of how serious their interest is. A major industry player and strong candidate partner company always will insist on exclusive rights. If they are going to make a major commitment to a business project, they want to make sure only their company reaps the benefits and not their competitors. If they do not clamor for exclusive rights, that is a major red flag, and U.S. executives should remove that company from consideration.

> If they do not clamor for exclusive rights, U.S. executives should remove that company from consideration.

(12) **Project launch:** The scale of the project launch the potential Asian partner is proposing to officially commence

the business in their market reflects their interest, commitment, financial involvement, and corporate capabilities. Examine where the company proposes to conduct the launch, whom they are planning to invite, and the length of the event.

For example, is it a ninety-minute ceremony inside their company and only employees are invited? Is it a half-day affair that takes place in the grand ballroom of one of the major hotels in the capital of their country with leaders from government, business, the media, and the community invited and involved? Furthermore, will they have only one launch program or will they hold launch events in several major cities? The greater the project launch planned, the greater their interest, commitment, and expectations are for the business.

(13) **Manufacturer or sales company:** It is important to know if the prospective partner is a manufacturer or if they are a sales company only. With potential partner companies that are manufacturers, there is always the inherent risk that they will incorporate knowledge of foreign products into their own product line and eventually produce or sell products that will compete—if not directly then indirectly through affiliates or companies where they have "cooperative relationships." Companies that are sales companies only are safer in that regard.

(14) **Banks:** In many Asian markets, company profiles list the bank(s) where a company does business. The rank and status of those banks is indicative of the company's financial strength and reputation in their domestic market. A country's better banks work with their country's better companies. So, if money-center banks in an Asian country do not collaborate with a local company, U.S. executives should be extra cautious in partnering with them.

(15) **Motivation:** Potential partner companies in international markets have any number of motivations for wanting to work with an American company in their domestic market, including gaining the opportunity to work with a leading foreign company to enlarge their market share, expand sales and profit, and increase their standing in their domestic industry. These, of course, are desirable motivations U.S. executives seek in partner companies overseas. However, there are several other reasons why companies in foreign markets want to work with American firms, and those reasons are not at all in your interests. The following are four of the more noteworthy reasons I have seen at play:

> Potential partner companies in international markets have any number of motivations for wanting to work with an American company.

- Obtaining and benefitting from the proprietary knowhow or intellectual property belonging to a U.S. company

- Securing a business agreement with a prominent American company as a source of great pride

  Becoming the partner of a leading foreign company provides an overseas company with bragging rights among their peers in their domestic industry. I call these "trophy rights" since the company is motivated more by the prestige of saying they are working with such and such a foreign company than in actually developing the business. Such companies collect business agreements on their corporate mantel as if they were trophies.

- Securing the business rights to a well-known U.S. company's products to help establish their company as the market leader among their domestic competitors

- Tying up the foreign company to *keep it out* of the international market

In these cases, often the overseas company is planning on launching or is already selling a similar product line either themselves or through a related company so they drag their feet during the negotiations, during the process to obtain government approval to import and sell your product, and during the roll out and sales of the product. The overseas company engages only in minimal marketing and sales efforts on behalf of the U.S. product. American companies can lose several years of investment, opportunity, market share, and profit as a result.

Clearly these four motivations are not in the interests of American companies. U.S. executives need to be extra diligent in ascertaining the motivation of companies they are screening. International business consultants, lawyers, and other industry experts are in a position to assist with this.

Partner selection is perhaps the most important decision U.S. executives must make in commencing business internationally, and negotiating provides the initial and critically important opportunity to screen and select a partner. When American companies work with the wrong partner company, they can pay a huge cost in terms of time, capital, energy, corporate image, product reputation, competitiveness, momentum,

> Negotiating provides the initial opportunity to screen and select a partner.

and lost sales and profit. In Asian markets, there is one additional negative consequence of selecting the wrong partner.

Generally speaking, Asian companies do not look favorably on foreign companies changing business partners there. In their view, changing business partners means a relationship breakdown or other major problem occurred.

> American companies need to get it right the first time when selecting their international business partners.

Consequently, American companies need to make careful decisions to get it right the first time when selecting their international business partners. U.S. executives will find that working closely with industry experts in evaluating and selecting their partners for international markets pays off many times over in the long run.

B. SEEK A PARTNER, NOT A DISTRIBUTOR

U.S. companies tend to frame their search for a company to work with in a foreign market in terms of finding a good sales company or distributor there. However, that is a strategic

> The key to maximizing success internationally is to work with a partner.

misstep as maximum success potential is rarely achieved by working with a sales company or distributor in international markets. The key to maximizing success internationally is to work with a partner.

What is the difference between a distributor and a partner? A distributor is solely interested in selling as many units of a given product as possible during the life of the sales cycle. While product sales represent the entirety of interest for a distributor, sales are but one part of the interest of a partner. Product sales are equally important to a partner; however, a partner views your business as an integral part of their own business. Accordingly, they also focus on the strategic dimensions of what is needed to maximize a foreign company's success in their market. That means establishing the foreign company's corporate image, company brand, unique technology, and product line as a leader in its industry segment for the long term.

Furthermore, when initial sales levels begin to drop off, a distributor shifts some, if not all, of its interest and efforts to selling other products that sell better. A distributor's level of commitment to selling a product is tied to that product's level of sales. As sales diminish, so does distributor commitment, focus, investment, and attention. In contrast, a partner is committed to both product sales and the mutual relationship with the foreign company. The two provide buoyance for each other, so if sales slow down, relational commitment and strategic interest keep a partner focused on the business project.

This is a powerful difference between a partner and a

distributor in Asia and a significant benefit that a partner brings to foreign executives. In addition, this dynamic illustrates that while relationship building and maintenance in Asian markets may cost American companies additional time and effort, the business payoffs are tangible and well worth the investment.

The following are seven additional major aspects that a partner provides to a foreign company that a distributor does not:

- A partner values your product concept, not just profiting from the sale of your product.

- A partner values the uniqueness, competitive advantage, and long-term sales potential of your product along with its underlying concept and technology. As a result, they formulate and commit their corporate resources to a business plan for your product line in their market that promotes not only your product but also its underlying concept and technology, and they do so for the long term.

- Your company's total success in their market is a major priority for a partner company. This is evidenced in
    o The number and quality of management and staff they assign to your project.
    o The amount of capital they commit to promoting your business.
    o The level and frequency of promotional activities they engage in for your project.

- A partner ensures that your product and its

underlying concept are properly understood in the market. They achieve that objective by engaging in appropriate marketing and educational activities on a regular basis throughout the market, including product usage workshops designed for both those selling the products and for product end-users. They do so at their expense.

- A partner respects and vigorously helps you defend your intellectual property. That means they take the lead in identifying and going after companies that infringe on your intellectual property.

- A partner actively updates you on competitive developments in their market that impact your business and proactively seeks new strategies and solutions to best deal with them in real time.

- A partner will go out of their way to find suggestions for you to improve your product so it can have greater appeal—and sales—in their market over the long term.

When a U.S. company selects a distributor to work with in an international market, it is equivalent to the American firm starting its business there in the batter's box trying to get a hit and get on first base. When an American company has a partner that is fully committed to going to bat for the U.S. company, the American firm starts its business there on second base.

The significance Asian companies place on relationship in business is discussed in numerous contexts and examples throughout this book. The center of that approach is that business is relationship based and driven. As discussed, this dimension of Asian business brings with it additional expectations and requirements, including the need to be committed to the mutual business relationship and business project for the long term. This trait is significantly stronger with a partner than a distributor.

I highly recommend that American executives take advantage of the traits of a partner company and the requirements of Asia's business culture to advance their business interests by selecting a company to work with that is a full-fledged partner and not just a distributor. By doing so, American executives can benefit from the requirements of Asia's business culture by leveraging those requirements to advance their own business interests instead of having the requirements be a burden or work against their interests. By being aware of and strategically navigating Asia's business cultures, U.S. executives can better ensure their success in Asian markets is both optimal and long term.

IV. THE RIGHT PEOPLE TO REPRESENT YOUR BUSINESS

A U.S. company's finding the right people for its business venture in Asia applies not only to selecting the most suitable in-country company to work with but also to selecting the right employees within its own company—those who are likely to do well working in Asian markets. Having the right members for the company's Asia team is critical; it will directly impact just about every facet of negotiating and business there including the following five areas:

- How smoothly its negotiating and overall experience of doing business in Asia proceed

- How productive its relationship is with international partners

- How effective its communication is with its partners in Asia

- How strong and long term the Asian partner's commitment to the business is over time

- Whether the U.S. company achieves maximum success, mediocre success, minimal success, or outright fails in Asian markets

> The best performing employees in the States can cause the greatest harm to the business interests of American companies abroad.

What are the right types of employees American companies need to have on their team for Asia? Contrary to what foreign executives often believe, the employees who get the best results in Asian markets are not necessarily the company's best performers in the domestic U.S. market. In fact, the best performing employees in the States can turn out to be the ones who have the hardest time in Asia and cause the greatest harm to the business interests of American companies abroad. The reason is that their domestic market success often acts as blinders that make it difficult to acknowledge and navigate the differences in the practice of Asian negotiating and business.

The ideal candidates for an American company's Asia team have the following characteristics. They are aware of—and accepting of—other cultures. They are flexible and realize that there is more than one way to engage in a task or achieve a goal. While they possess confidence, they are not insistent on their own way of doing things but rather are patient with and open-minded regarding different approaches to negotiating and communication. They realize that just as there is more than one train to take them to a destination, there can be more than one way things are done in any given market. The proverbial bull in the china closet is precisely the person you do *not* want involved in your international business.

At least one member of your Asia team needs to be experienced in the local Asian markets of interest. If a potential member of your Asia team has had previous experience working there, make sure that experience is not out of date. I have worked with clients who hired such professionals and witnessed numerous times how their way of conducting business was not only unsuccessful but even detrimental. Experience needs to be qualified in terms of how recent, relevant, and strong it is relative to your company's specific needs and objectives.

As discussed in chapter five, your company needs to have your own *facilitator interpreter* on your team to provide accurate cultural interpretation as well as linguistic translation. This person can advance corporate goals and business interests by bridging the differing business practices and inherent but unspoken expectations between America and Asian countries. He or she can ensure that your company successfully navigates Asia's culture-based differences in business practices so that instead of those differences hindering your firm's results, those differences can be intentionally and strategically leveraged to enhance your success in Asian markets.

Having meaningful Asian market business experience and cultural fluency within your Asia team is a powerful catalyst that American executives need to have when negotiating and commencing the process of doing business in Asia. When you do, it is comparable to having both the correct address in the target Asian market and a GPS system to take you where you want to go; the company knows its destination and has the right tool to get it there without ending up taking detours, getting lost, going down dead-end streets, or having misspent time and expenses. U.S. executives who do not have these assets on their company team only have an address; they may know where they want to go in an international market but have no idea how to get there and are unaware of the obstacles and pitfalls that await along the way. In effect, they are driving blind.

It is important to note that Asian companies will evaluate and want to have a comfort level with executives representing foreign firms on three distinct levels:

- **Who you are as an individual:** This includes your character and how easy you are to work with.

- **Who you are as a professional:** This incorporates whether or not you conduct business in a timely, professional, and ethical manner.

- **Who you are as a representative of your company:** Are you of sufficient rank, from an appropriate department in your firm, and fully knowledgeable about your firm's business and the current negotiation? Sending the assistant director of human resources in your firm to negotiate a major manufacturing agreement, for example, would not be favorably viewed.

I have always found Asian markets to be very unforgiving; businesses are expected to get it right the first time. In the States, not succeeding is often viewed as a learning experience to do it better in the future. However, in Asia not succeeding is considered to be the result of insufficient preparation. So, it is important that American companies select the right people to represent them from the outset. This is especially true in negotiating, where the Asian market's relationship requirements present an additional level of challenge that is not present in the States.

> I have always found Asian markets to be very unforgiving; businesses are expected to get it right the first time.

Changing members of your negotiating team is not viewed favorably in Asia. It is thought of as interfering with the flow and momentum of the discussions. More importantly, as relationship building is such an essential facet of negotiating, personnel changes impede and complicate this. This is especially true in China where negotiating occurs more on a person-to-person level than a company-to-company level, as discussed in chapter two. Given this negotiating dynamic in China, personnel changes are seen as an opportunity to revisit previously negotiated items that did not turn out quite the way the Chinese company had hoped. A replacement negotiator representing an American company is viewed by Chinese negotiators as a fresh opportunity to renegotiate what they want, as the new person might be more amenable to the Chinese position.

Seniority and rank are very important in negotiating in Asian countries. It would create a negative perception if a low or midlevel manager was sent to lead negotiation discussions with companies in Asia. Asian executives would tend to react by feeling insulted and assume that the U.S. company was not serious about the business project. Make sure you know who the highest-level executive is on the Asian company's negotiating team and that your highest-ranking company representative is of at least comparable rank.

Last, it is highly advisable to determine how the names of your company executives who will lead your negotiating team translate into the language of the international market. To share a client example in the Japanese market, the name of the international sales director of the U.S. firm was Joe Dunn. While a name common in the States, in Japanese the name has the same pronunciation as the word for "joke"—*jou-dan* (冗談). Japanese executives would often be embarrassed as they sought not to laugh upon hearing his name for the first time and would later jest about it. An American company being represented by a senior executive—in this case, its international sales director—who introduces himself by saying "Hello, my name is Mr. Joke" is probably not the ideal image you want your company to project when trying to succeed in highly competitive foreign markets.

V. ORGANIZATIONAL IMPEDIMENTS

In my years as a management consultant and now as an international business advisor, I have always been amazed at how successful businesses are *in spite of themselves*. Despite inefficiencies, ineffective management, poor performance, and other self-created obstacles impeding optimal success, better companies tend to continue doing well. Such organizational impediments are found in companies' negotiating just as they are in other areas of business.

Organizational impediments in negotiating are factors found within the company that hinder optimal success in negotiating. Differing from company to company and being too numerous to cover here, the purpose of this section is to alert the reader to their existence and hopefully prompt executives to review their own businesses to identify and eliminate them as part of preparing for negotiations.

The following seven are some of the more common impediments to negotiating that I have come across:

- The goals of the negotiation are not fully in line with the strategic interests of the company. No matter how skillful the negotiator may be, if the end result of a negotiation is not on track for advancing the interests of the company, optimal negotiation success is not feasible.

- Poor communication, competition, or rivalry between the company's departments can result in the company engaging in negotiations without the sufficient knowledge of other company departments. Consequently, not all of the departments relevant to a negotiation are participating in or even aware of it, causing problems when it comes time to implement the terms of the negotiation.

- The department spearheading a negotiation believes that other departments, if involved, would push for terms or conditions different from or unfavorable to itself.

- Personal ambitions of the head of the department can interfere with outcome when personal or departmental achievement is put above the overall interests of the organization.

- Negotiations are impeded when there is insufficient knowledge of and/or experience with:
  o the topic under negotiation.
  o the differing industry conditions in the target country.
  o the different market conditions in the target country.
  o the different regulatory requirements of the Asian market.
  o the company one is negotiating with.
  o the cultural differences that underpin the negotiating dynamics of the international market.

- A firm's internal corporate culture is not conducive to effectively dealing with the cultural differences that inform the negotiating dynamics of the international market.

- Management lacks the interest or staying power to meet the long-term commitment and orientation required in Asian markets.

Each of these is a critically important facet of negotiating in international markets. Lack of knowledge in any of these areas greatly impacts the degree of success American firms achieve and can cost significant amounts of time, effort, capital, and resources.

INSIGHTS

Negotiating is the gateway to significant opportunity in international markets for companies of any size. As negotiating is conducted differently from country to country and culture to culture, a cookie cutter approach to negotiation rarely produces optimal success. While the categories of differences American executives are challenged by may bear similarities from market to market, the specific, esoteric remedies for each international market will be unique. In order not to limit or outright prevent their success, U.S. executives need to be aware of and adequately prepared to deal with these specific differences in the practice of negotiating around the world.

As we have seen throughout this book, negotiating in Asia presents American executives with a distinct set of dissimilarities and challenges ranging from differing approaches, dynamics, and protocols to communication styles to far-reaching relationship considerations to unique market needs. The focus of this book has been to illustrate the differences in conducting negotiations between America and Asia as well as to examine negotiating differences among the nations of the Far East. It is the hope of this author that this three-dimensional analysis, based on nearly four decades of first-hand experience, will serve as a practical guide to better prepare and enable American companies to succeed in international and intercultural negotiations.

Bibliography

About the Author

Representative Client Evaluations

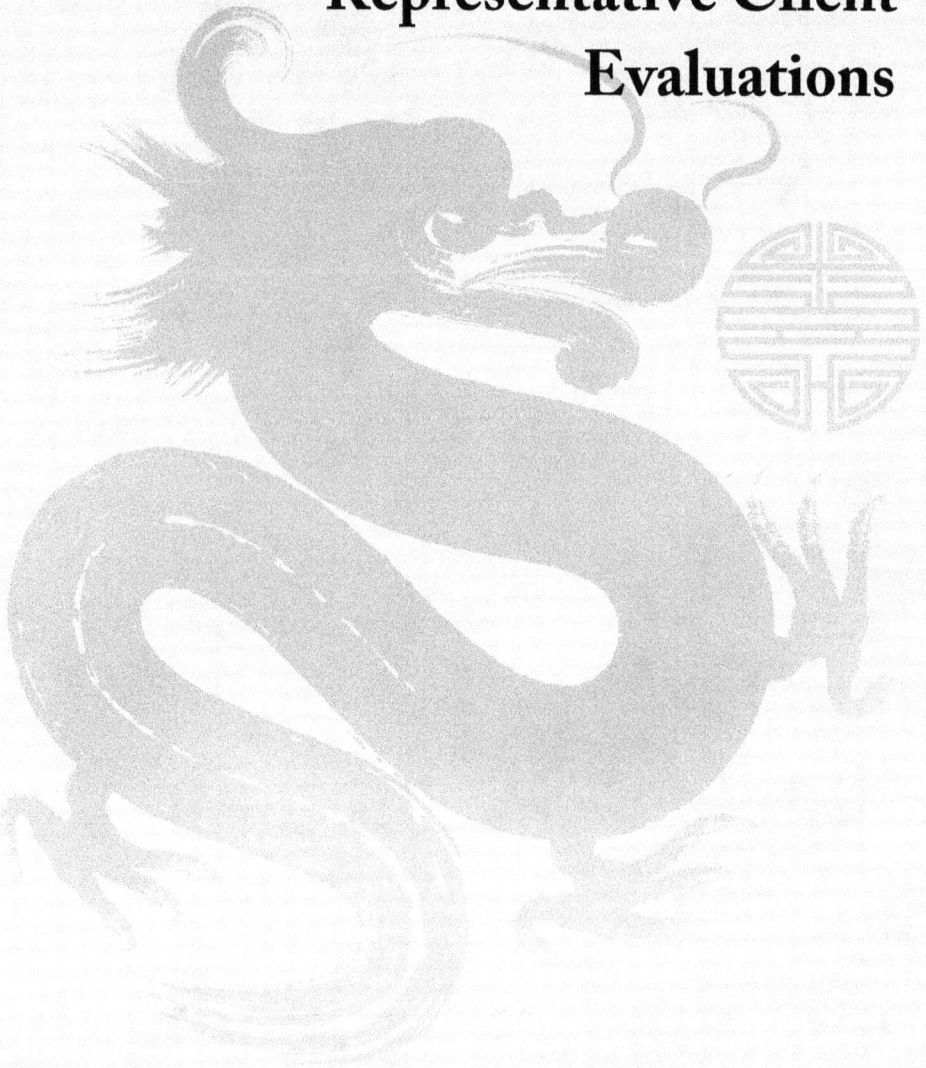

BIBLIOGRAPHY

There is a dearth of recent publications on Asian negotiating. While some of the following may be dated, they are nonetheless noteworthy.

Azar, Robert Charles. *Navigating Japan's Business Culture: A Practical Guide to Succeeding in the Japanese Market.* Raleigh, NC: Write Way Publishing Company, 2016.

Blaker, Michael, Paul Giarra, and Ezra Vogel. *Case Studies in Japanese Negotiating Behavior.* Washington, DC: United States Institute of Peace, 2002.

Brett, Jeanne M. *Negotiating Globally.* San Francisco, CA: Josey-Bass, 2014.

Cellich, Claude and Subhash C. Jain. *Practical Solutions to Global Business Negotiations.* New York: Business Expert Press, 2012.

Cohen, Raymond. *Negotiating Across Cultures: International Communication in an Interdependent World.* Washington, DC: U.S. Institute of Peace, 2002.

Condon, John C. *With Respect to the Japanese.* Tokyo, Japan: Yohan Publications, Inc., 1984.

Drucker, Peter F. *The Essential Drucker.* New York: Harper Collins, 2001.

"Peter F. Drucker Quotes" Goodreads. https://www.goodreads.com/author/quotes/12008.Peter_F_Drucker July 7, 2018.

Fisher, Roger and William Ury. *Getting to Yes: Negotiating Agreement Without Giving In.* New York: Penguin Books, 2011.

Government of Japan. *We are Tomodachi (We are Friends).* Tokyo: Office of the Prime Minister, Spring/Summer 2014.

Harvard Business Essentials. *Negotiation.* Boston, MA: Harvard Business Review Press, 2003.

Inamori, Kazuo. *A Compass to Fulfillment: Passion and Spirituality in Life and Business.* New York: McGraw Hill, 2010.

Katz, Lothar. *Negotiating International Business.* Charleston, SC: Booksurge, LLC, 2006.

March, Robert M. *The Japanese Negotiator: Subtlety and Strategy Beyond Western Logic.* New York: Kodansha International, 1988.

March, Robert M. and Su-Hua Wu. *The Chinese Negotiator: How to Succeed in the World's Largest Market.* Tokyo, Japan: Kodansha International, 2007.

Nixon, Peter. *Mastering Business in Asia: Negotiating.* Singapore: John Wiley & Sons (Asia) Pte. Ltd., 2005.

PHP Institute, Inc. *Matsushita Konosuke: His Life & Legacy.* Tokyo: PHP Institute, Inc., 1994.

QuotesWise: Akio Morita. http://www.quoteswise.com/akio-morita-quotes-2.html.

Requejo, William Hernandez and John L. Graham. *Global Negotiating: The New Rules.* New York: Palgrave Macmillan, 2008.

Salacuse, Jeswald W. *The Global Negotiator: Making, Managing, and Mending Deals Around the World in the Twenty-First Century.* New York: Palgrave Macmillan, 2003.

Solomon, Richard H. *Chinese Negotiating Behavior: Pursuing Interests Through "Old Friends.'* Washington, DC: U.S. Institute of Peace, 2005.

Solomon, Richard H. and Nigel Quinney. *American Negotiating Behavior: Wheeler-Dealers, Legal Eagles, Bullies and Preachers.* Washington, DC: United States Institute of Peace, 2011.

Voss, Chris with Tahl Raz. *Never Split the Difference: Negotiating as if Your Life Depended On It.* New York: Harper Business, 2016.

Weiss, Jeff. *HBR Guide to Negotiating.* Boston, MA: Harvard Business Review Press, 2016.

ABOUT THE AUTHOR

Robert Charles Azar

Robert Azar is a U.S.-Asia business and cultural expert with nearly forty years of executive level success. As a strategy advisor, he specializes in achieving excellence in global business development, problem resolution, and intercultural management.

Mr. Azar is one of only 10,000 consultants in the U.S. to have earned the Certified Management Consultant (CMC) designation, the management consulting industry's preeminent recognition for demonstrated achievements and excellence in client satisfaction, professional standards, and ethical business practices.

He lived in the Far East for seven years, worked in Asian corporations at the management level for ten years, and developed and managed U.S. and European businesses in Asian markets for over twenty-five years. He reads, writes, and speaks Japanese fluently and is familiar with the Korean language.

Mr. Azar was honored to attend the White House's

welcome ceremony for Japanese Prime Minister Abe Shinzo for U.S.-Japan trade discussions on April 28, 2015. He was one of four hundred leaders in U.S.-Asian affairs to attend President Clinton's major policy speech before his summit meeting with then-Chinese President Jiang Zemin in Washington, D.C. on October 24, 1997.

Prior to commencing his career in international business and intercultural management, Mr. Azar completed a decade of formal academic training and field research in Asian politics, economics, and culture. His double major BA degree in International Relations and East Asian Studies from New York University led to completing an MA degree in East Asian political, economic, and cultural affairs at Columbia University. He then studied international marketing, global management, and business law at Harvard University. *Negotiating in Asia* is his third book. He also is the published author of numerous articles and reports on U.S.-Asian business, economics, foreign policy, and culture, published both in America and Japan, in English and in Japanese.

As an expert on Asia, Mr. Azar has been interviewed frequently by major international media for more than thirty-five years. He has been a guest on CNN, CNBC, the Financial News Network (FNN), the Wall Street Journal Report as well as on local cable television and radio shows in the United States. In Japan, he has appeared, speaking in Japanese, on Television Tokyo's "World Business Satellite" (Japan's foremost business news program), NHK, Nippon Television, Fuji Television, and numerous radio shows. He has also been featured in several interviews in leading American and Asian news publications, including *The New York Times*, *Business Week*, *Crain's BtoB*, and *Kenko Sangyo Shimbun* (Health Industry News).

His international career spans numerous industries and several fields of global business, including strategic planning, negotiating, management, finance, intercultural mediation, global business development, international sales and marketing, market research, international trade, product development, human resource management, trouble shooting, turn around services, and political and economic analysis—in both the for-profit and the non-profit sectors.

Mr. Azar has extensive experience in advising companies seeking to succeed in Asian markets. He is often called upon to speak, present, and teach on U.S.-Asian business and cultural matters to corporate, government, academic, and cultural entities. An adjunct professor, he teaches global business at the SKEMA Business School and management at Elon University.

He has served as a member of the board of directors for numerous organizations, including the World Trade Council, Institute of Management Consultants, American Cancer Society, the North Carolina Japan Center, United Arts Council of Wake County, and the Japanese Center for Quality of Life Studies.

Mr. Azar has logged over a million flight miles traveling to, from, and within Asia. He is a collector of Asian art and antique ceramics and paints Japanese calligraphy.

He currently serves as president of Asia Strategic Advisors LLC®, a company that teaches and advises U.S. businesses, government agencies, cultural institutions, and non-profit organizations on achieving optimal success doing business with Asian entities operating either in Asia or America. For further information, see AsiaStrategicAdvisors.com.

REPRESENTATIVE CLIENT EVALUATIONS

"It has been my distinct privilege to work with Robert Azar on many different projects and in many different capacities off and on over the past 30 years. The depth and breadth of Mr. Azar's experience in doing business in Asia is truly staggering. I cannot think of any non-Japanese person who understands the language and culture of Japan better than Mr. Azar.

"It is this unique and thorough understanding of culture that enables Mr. Azar to help his clients and business partners to succeed in Japan and other Asian markets. He is also a man of integrity. I am pleased to recommend Mr. Azar to anyone looking to expand their business success in Asia." — **Paul Taylor, Esq., Vice President & General Counsel, Ajinomoto North America, Inc., Portland, Oregon, U.S.A.**

"With your assistance, we were able to increase our sales by 70% last year! A good percentage of our growth is attributed to your efforts in Asia. We anticipate, with your help, to continue to expand these markets and increase our sales even further." — **Marty Davidson, President & CEO, Excel Cosmeceuticals, Inc., Bloomfield Hills, Minnesota, U.S.A.**

"Koken Co., Ltd. has had the opportunity to work closely with Mr. Robert C. Azar over the past two years. We have found him to be an individual of utmost integrity and professionalism. Mr. Azar's knowledge of the Japanese health and skin care market is unsurpassed, even by our own executives.

"In addition to impeccable Japanese language skills, his ability to resolve difficulties encountered in doing business internationally is outstanding. It is without hesitation that I unconditionally recommend Robert Azar." — **Teruo Miyata, Ph.D., President & CEO, Koken Co., Ltd., Tokyo, Japan**

"These sales are really good news. Thanks for believing in us....You are a true hero! Congrats!" — **Arnd Kensy, President & Ulrich Tobies, Director of International Sales, Human Med AG, Berlin, Germany**

"I have known Robert Azar for several years now and worked closely with him when he was engaged to provide services to Obagi Medical Products. Robert is highly skilled in launching brands globally and building an international presence.

"In one particular project, I worked with Robert to bring the Obagi brand to Japan. In the process of completing that project, it was very clear that Robert had extensive knowledge of the medical channels in Japan, who the key opinion leaders are, what companies had the largest market share, the best reputation and/or the highest growth rates, as well as who the best potential distribution partners would be for Obagi. Further, the key opinion leaders and industry players in Japan knew Robert, and it became clear that he has garnered excellent relationships throughout that country and many others.

"One of my existing contacts in Japan noted, after speaking with Robert, that he was very surprised that Robert was not Japanese - which is a testament to Robert's absolutely flawless command of the Japanese language and his natural understanding/competency with cultural norms and subtleties. Finding someone with these skills is rare - but adding those skills to his sharp business acumen and industry knowledge sets Robert even further apart. Top qualities: Great results, expert, high integrity.

"In short, Robert is a proven professional that delivered on all of the projects that we engaged him on and I would welcome the opportunity to work with Robert again, anywhere in the world." — **Curtis Cluff, Former CFO, Obagi Medical Products, Inc., Long Beach, California, U.S.A.**

"I had the sincere pleasure of working with Robert Azar for many years at Obagi Medical. He was a life-saver.

"Robert assisted me in breaking into many Asian Markets–Japan and Korea notably. His understanding of the physician channel, those companies/distributers who had the largest market-share in that channel and the key opinion leaders within those markets provided Obagi quick access and success.

Robert's command of the Japanese language, his ability to understand the objectives of his clients, and his superior knowledge of the international market, make him one of the best all-round professionals that I have met in the industry, to date. I would welcome and look forward to the opportunity of working with Robert again." — **Kathleen LaGrave, Former Director, International Sales, Obagi Medical Products, Inc., Long Beach, California, U.S.A.**

"Having worked with Robert Azar for over two-and-a-half years, I must say that he is very much involved in helping grow markets for American companies wishing to add sales outlets in Asia and Europe.

"Mr. Azar is fluent in Japanese, which is very rare for an American, and I have found that to be an invaluable asset in promoting product sales in Japan. He also has very good contacts in Korea, China, and other parts of Asia, and excellent relationships with sub-distributors throughout the area. He has a vast knowledge of International Markets in general and a specific knowledge of various Asian cultures. And his focus on strategic sales is both unique and beneficial.

"I would definitely recommend Mr. Azar to anyone wanting to enter the International Market." — **William Kelly, Director of International Sales, Sciton Inc., Palo Alto, California, U.S.A.**

"I have known Robert Azar for a couple of years now. I worked very closely with him when he successfully introduced Brava AFT System in the Japanese market. His quick progress into the Japanese market proved us correct in trusting Robert with this delicate operation. Robert is highly skilled in finding the best strategy for your medical device in the Japanese market. He has vast knowledge of the medical device industry in Japan, from manufacturers to distributors, and end users. His understanding of the language and the culture along with his business experience in Japan makes him one of the best in launching products in this market. Robert has been a trustworthy business partner. I am pleased to recommend Robert to anyone looking to expand their business success in Japan." — **Ercan Dilsen, VP Operations, Brava, LLC, Miami, Florida, U.S.A.**

www.ingramcontent.com/pod-product-compliance
Lightning Source LLC
Chambersburg PA
CBHW061135220326
41599CB00025B/4240